W9-BWF-929

Published by:

Frommer Media LLC

Copyright © 2019 FrommerMedia LLC, New York, NY. All rights reserved. No part of this publication may be reproduced, stored in a retrieval system or transmitted in any form or by any means, electronic, mechanical, photocopying, recording, scanning or otherwise, except as permitted under Sections 107 or 108 of the 1976 United States Copyright Act, without the prior written permission of the Publisher. Requests to the Publisher for permission should be addressed to Support@FrommerMedia.com.

ISBN: 978-1-628-87448-8 (paper); 978-1-628-87449-5 (ebk)

Editorial Director: Pauline Frommer
Development Editor: Alexis Lipsitz Flippin
Production Editor: Kelly Dobbs Henthorne
Photo Editor: Meghan Lamb
Assistant Photo Editor: Phil Vinke
Cartographer: Roberta Stockwell
Indexer: Kelly Dobbs Henthorne

Front cover photos, left to right: Alfama District © ESB Professional; Monument to the Discoveries at Belém, Lisbon © Photo and Vector / Shutterstock.com; Street musicians play jazz and folk music at city square © Elena Dijour / Shutterstock.com.

Back cover photo: Vintage tram in Lisbon © S-F.

For information on our other products and services, please go to Frommers.com.

Frommer's also publishes its books in a variety of electronic formats. Some content that appears in print may not be available in electronic formats.

Manufactured in China

5   4   3   2   1

About This Guide

Organizing your time. That's what this guide is all about.

Other guides give you long lists of things to see and do and then expect you to fit the pieces together. The Day by Day guides are different. These guides tell you the best of everything, and then they show you how to see it *in the smartest, most time-efficient way*. Our authors have designed detailed itineraries organized by time, neighborhood, or special interest. And each tour comes with a bulleted map that takes you from stop to stop.

Hoping to get a little lost strolling the ancient cobbled streets of Lisbon's historic Alfama? Is a night of dancing to the soulful rhythms of *fado* music on your bucket list? Craving to see the magnificent panorama of Lisbon from its *miradouros*, viewpoints high above the city? Whatever your interest or schedule, the Day by Day guides give you the smartest routes to follow. Not only do we take you to the top attractions, hotels, and restaurants, but we also help you access those special moments that locals get to experience—those "finds" that turn tourists into travelers.

The Day by Days are also your top choice if you're looking for one complete guide for all your travel needs. The best hotels and restaurants for every budget, the greatest shopping values, the wildest nightlife—it's all here.

Why should you trust our judgment? Because our authors personally visit each place they write about. They're an independent lot who say what they think and would never include places they wouldn't recommend to their best friends. They're also open to suggestions from readers. If you'd like to contact them, please send your comments our way at feedback@frommers.com, and we'll pass them on.

Enjoy your Day by Day guide—the most helpful travel companion you can buy. And have the trip of a lifetime.

About the Author

Paul Ames has been enchanted by Portugal since he first arrived as a child in 1975 and found the country gripped by revolutionary ferver. He lives in Lisbon, works as a freelance journalist, and never tires of exploring the delights of his adopted homeland from the vine-covered hills of the Minho to Madeira's rocky shores and all the beaches in between.

An Additional Note

Please be advised that travel information is subject to change at any time—and this is especially true of prices. We therefore suggest that you write or call ahead for confirmation when making your travel plans. The authors, editors, and publisher cannot be held responsible for the experiences of readers while traveling. Your safety is important to us, however, so we encourage you to stay alert and be aware of your surroundings.

Star Ratings, Icons & Abbreviations

Every hotel, restaurant, and attraction listing in this guide has been ranked for quality, value, service, amenities, and special features using a **star-rating system.** Hotels, restaurants, attractions, shopping, and nightlife are rated on a scale of zero stars (recommended) to three stars (exceptional). In addition to the star-rating system, we also use a **kids icon** to point out the best bets for families. Within each tour, we recommend cafes, bars, or restaurants where you can take a break. Each of these stops appears in a shaded box marked with a coffee-cup-shaped bullet ☕.

The following **abbreviations** are used for credit cards:

AE	American Express	MC	MasterCard
DC	Diners Club	V	Visa

Travel Resources at Frommers.com

Now that you have this guidebook to help you plan a great trip, visit our website at **www.frommers.com** for additional travel information on more than 4,000 destinations. We update features regularly to give you instant access to the most current trip-planning information available. At Frommers.com, you'll find scoops on the best airfares, lodging rates, and car rental bargains. You can even book your travel online through our reliable travel booking partners. Other popular features include:

- Online updates of our most popular guidebooks
- Vacation sweepstakes and contest giveaways
- Newsletters highlighting the hottest travel trends
- Online travel message boards with featured travel discussions

A Note on Prices

In the "Take a Break" and "Best Bets" sections of this book, we have used a system of dollar signs to show a range of costs for 1 night in a hotel (the price of a double-occupancy room) or the cost of an entree at a restaurant. Use the following table to decipher the dollar signs:

Cost	Hotels	Restaurants
$	under $100	under $10
$$	$100–$200	$10–$200
$$$	$200–$300	$20–$30
$$$$	$300–$400	$30–$40
$$$$$	over $400	over $40

An Invitation to the Reader

In researching this book, we discovered many wonderful places—hotels, restaurants, shops, and more. We're sure you'll find others. Please tell us about them, so we can share the information with your fellow travelers in upcoming editions. If you were disappointed with a recommendation, we'd love to know that, too. Please write to: Support@FrommerMedia.com.

Frommer's

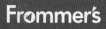

Lisbon

day BY day®

3rd Edition

Ames

FrommerMedia LLC

Contents

10 Favorite
Moments

10 Favorite Moments

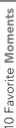

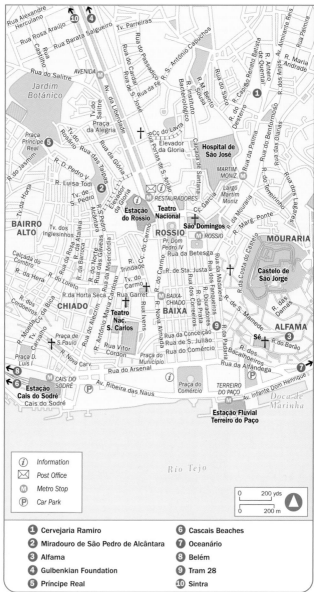

	Information
$\boxtimes$	Post Office
Ⓜ	Metro Stop
Ⓟ	Car Park

1	Cervejaria Ramiro	6	Cascais Beaches
2	Miradouro de São Pedro de Alcântara	7	Oceanário
3	Alfama	8	Belém
4	Gulbenkian Foundation	9	Tram 28
5	Príncipe Real	10	Sintra

Previous page: Lisbon skyline.

Portugal's maritime capital has been open to the world since its explorers and spice traders reached across the oceans in the 15th century. Today, Lisbon is changing fast as booming tourism fills medieval alleys with hip hotels, chic eateries, and fashionable stores. Yet the city's soul lives on in the plaintive sound of *fado* music, the character of its historic neighborhoods, and the eternal embrace of the River Tagus. It all adds up a heady cocktail of art and architecture, vibrant street life, and cafe culture, bathed in almost year-round sunshine.

1 Tucking into superlative seafood. The world is waking up to the delights of Portuguese cuisine. Based on seafood freshly caught along the country's long Atlantic seaboard, the traditional cooking is simple, but delicious. One of the biggest treats is eating chargrilled bream or bass accompanied by local wine as you look out over the glassy waters of the Tagus. Or try a shellfish extravaganza washed down with iced beer at a bustling *marisqueira* (seafood restaurant). See p 105.

2 Taking in the views from rooftops and miradouros. They say that Lisbon, like Rome, is built on seven hills. The ups and downs are tiring for calf muscles but rewarding for the eyes. The city is sprinkled with *miradouros* (viewing points) offering glorious vistas. Favorites include São Pedro de Alcântara, looking across downtown to the castle of São Jorge or Portas do Sol perched above Alfama's rooftops and the Tagus beyond. Rooftop bars have sprouted on hotels, shopping malls, office blocks, and even parking lots so you can enjoy cocktails with the views. p 127.

3 Getting lost in Alfama and catching some fado. Lisbon's ancient heart is a tangle of cobbled streets and narrow steps. Getting lost amid its lanes is a delight. Discover tiny churches lined with blue-and-white *azulejos* (ceramic tiles), new street art, or pavement barbecues pungent with grilled sardines. On Tuesdays and Saturdays catch the sprawling Feira da Ladra (Thieves Market), a treasure

Diners toasting the vistas from the São Pedro de Alcântara miradouro.

trove of bric-à-brac. Alfama is also the spiritual home of *fado* music with its passionate love songs. See p 46.

4 Uncovering the art at the Gulbenkian Foundation. Lisbon's most influential arts institution is the legacy of an Armenian oil magnate who found refuge here during WWII. The Gulbenkian runs two museums: one dedicated to the founder's collection of treasures from Ancient Egypt to the French Impressionists; and the other a panorama of modern art. Located in a peaceful garden, the foundation also has a concert hall hosting its own symphony orchestra and visiting musicians. See p 128.

5 Shopping without dropping in Príncipe Real. This aristocratic uptown neighborhood has the chicest shopping. Arguably the world's prettiest mall is located in an Arabesque palace. Another is dedicated to designers from Brazil. Rows of tasteful, original boutiques line the streets. Take a break in some of the district's cool bars and cafes, or chill in leafy havens like Praça das Flores or Jardim do Príncipe Real. See p 79.

A street vendor grills sardines.

6 Topping up your tan on suburban sand. Hop on a train at waterfront Cais do Sodré station and you'll hit the beach in 15 minutes. From Caxias to Cascais a string of sandy coves boast calm waters and soft sand. Carcavelos is the grandest, a broad strand that's popular with surf schools and flanked by an imposing 16th-century fortress. A bit farther out are untouched coves bathed by Atlantic rollers, sheltered bays with turquoise water, and fun urban beaches fronted by cafes.

7 Going nose to nose with sharks. Lisbon's Oceanário showcases sea life in spectacular fashion, from a vast central tank where sharks, rays, and tuna patrol to ocean-themed sections where you can get up close to puffins, luminous jellyfish, and jewel-like seahorses. *See p 18.*

8 Marveling at the Manueline. The Mosteiro dos Jerónimos and Torre de Belém are pinnacles of a unique Portuguese architectural style named after King Manuel I, patron of the Discoveries. The UNESCO World Heritage buildings are the main attraction in the riverside Belém district—although the lines are sometimes even longer at Pastéis de Belém, a cafe serving custard-filled tarts since 1835. *See p 16.*

9 Making like a commuter on boats and trams. If your legs tire of those hills, hop on one of the little yellow streetcars that rattle around the narrow streets. Tram 28 is the most famed, but it gets crowded on its route through the most historic neighborhoods. Lines 14, 15, or 25 also offer a retro transport adventure. Or join commuters on one of the ferries heading to south-bank suburbs; the views make the trip worthwhile. *See p 10.*

10 Immersing yourself in Sintra's fantasy. Lord Byron called Sintra a "Glorious Eden." Amid forest-covered hills, romantic palaces rise among the trees. Two belonged to the royal family: one a Renaissance gem in town, the other a romantic hilltop confection dreamed up by a German prince. It's an inspirational fusion of art and nature. *See p 160.* ●

The sunset cityscape from the Belvedere of Our Lady of the Hill.

The Best in One Day

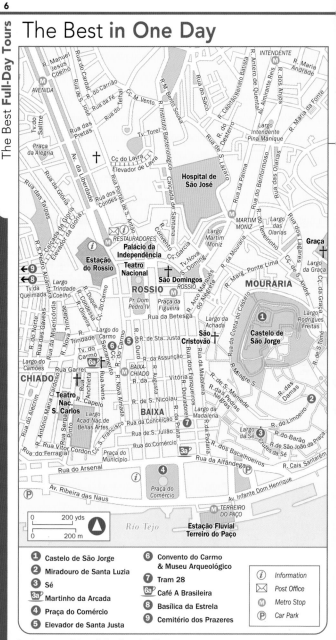

1 Castelo de São Jorge
2 Miradouro de Santa Luzia
3 Sé
3a Martinho da Arcada
4 Praça do Comércio
5 Elevador de Santa Justa
6 Convento do Carmo & Museu Arqueológico
7 Tram 28
6a Café A Brasileira
8 Basílica da Estrela
9 Cemitério dos Prazeres

ⓘ Information
✉ Post Office
Ⓜ Metro Stop
Ⓟ Car Park

Previous page: Lisbon skyline from the Alfama.

This full-day tour is an introduction to Portugal's historic capital. You'll get your bearings looking out from the hilltop citadel where the city was born in pre-Roman times. Then head down through its most characteristic neighborhoods: Alfama, the Baixa, and Chiado. The route roughly follows the rails of the iconic Tram 28, so you can hop on if the going gets tough on the feet. You can also make the tour in reverse if you want to beat the rush for the tram and catch sunset from the castle. START: **Castelo de São Jorge. Rua de Santa Cruz do Castelo. Bus: 737.**

Tram 28, which links several of Lisbon's historic districts.

① ★★★ kids **Castelo de São Jorge.** Phoenicians, Romans, and Visigoths lived here before Arabs from northern Africa built the stronghold that sits atop the highest of Lisbon's hills. More than 4 centuries of Muslim rule came to an end in 1147 when Portugal's first king, Afonso Henriques, enlisted the help of northern European crusaders, to besiege the city. Despite its bellicose history, the Castle of St. George is nowadays a peaceful place. Come in the early morning or evening when there are fewer visitors and it's more like a tranquil garden than a fortress. Pathways are shaded by venerable olive, pine and cork trees, peacocks hop among the ruins, and the views over the city and the shimmering waters of the Tagus are extraordinary.

This is the place to get your bearings on a first visit to Lisbon. Virtually the whole city is laid out before you, from the medieval alleyways beneath the ramparts to the regular 18th-century blocks of the Baixa district and gleaming modern towers atop the far hills. There's also plenty to see within the castle walls: an archeological site where secrets of past centuries are still being unearthed; a neat little **museum** showing the history of the castle through artifacts; and an odd *camera obscura* that uses a lens and looking glasses to zoom in on city landmarks. Kids will enjoy the Sunday re-enactments of battles and medieval pageantry, not to mention the after-dark tours to observe the castle's abundant **bat population.** There's a good restaurant, plus a range of snack options inside the castle. ⏱ *1 hr. Rua de Santa Cruz do Castelo.* ☎ *21/880-0620. www.castelodesaojorge.pt. Admission 8.50€ adults; 5€ seniors, disabled, and students under 25; free children 9 and under. Nov–Feb 9am–6pm; Mar–Oct 9am–9pm.*

② ★★ Miradouro de Santa Luzia.

Built atop seven hills, Lisbon does not lack for splendid viewpoints. Wander down among the charming lanes of the Castelo neighborhood to discover this one perched over the river. It's shaded by purple bougainvillea and surrounded by *azulejos*—Portugal's distinctive blue ceramic tiles. Below are the red rooftops of **Alfama,** the heart of the medieval city, ripe for exploring (see p 46). The panoramic viewpoint is backed by a pretty little church belonging to the knightly Order of Malta. Hidden behind it is a staircase leading to a little terrace bar with its own unique view over the city. ① 20 min. Tram: 12, 28. Bus: 737.

③ ★★ Sé (Cathedral).

Follow the tram tracks downhill to the bulky stone structure that has served as Lisbon's cathedral since the 1100s. There's a reason it looks more like a fortress than a place of worship: For decades following Lisbon's capture by Christians in 1147, churches were built to serve as defendable sanctuaries in event of a Muslim counterattack. Although damaged by the 1755 earthquake, the Sé remains an impressive example of the Romanesque style with its barrel-vaulted ceiling and arched upper-level gallery. Graceful Gothic additions were made in later centuries. Most notable are the airy **cloisters**, but restoration work means they are closed until at least 2020. ① 30 min. Largo da Sé. ☎ 21/886-6752. Free admission; cloisters 2.50€. Mon–Sat 9am–7pm; Sun 9am–8pm. Tram: 12, 28. Bus: 37.

③A ❷ Martinho da Arcada.

If it's time for a pitstop, head for this historic cafe, serving thirsty Lisboetas since 1778. There's a bar with a couple of tables for snacks and coffee, an elegant dining room out back serving classic Portuguese meals, and an esplanade under the arcades. It was once a hangout for the modernist poet Fernando Pessoa. *Praça do Comércio, 3 www.martinhoda arcada.pt.* ☎ 21/887-9259.

④ ★★ Praça do Comércio.

One of Europe's great urban spaces looks out onto the vast expanse of the Tagus estuary. This was the nerve center of the Portuguese maritime empire where ships would pull in from Africa, Asia, and the Americas. It was overseen by a grand royal palace. Although locals still call the square Terreiro do Paço ("palace courtyard"), the palace and the trade depots were destroyed by the great earthquake and tsunami of 1755. In its place were built the stately government buildings you see today. Two sturdy white towers bookend rows of pastel-painted ministries. At ground level are white-stone arcades sheltering cafes and restaurants. On one side is an interactive museum: the **Lisbon Story Centre** (www.lisbon storycentre.pt), explaining the city's history. In the center of the square

Lisbon's Sé Cathedral.

The Praça do Comércio.

is an imposing horseback statue of King José I (1714–77). Facing the river is a sculpture-laden triumphal arch, the **Arco da Rua Augusta,** which you can climb for a 2.5€ fee to enjoy 360-degree views over the city from over 100 feet up. Through the arch is **Rua Augusta,** a bustling pedestrianized thoroughfare that traverses the heart of the grid-plan **Baixa** district, laid out by the Marquês de Pombal, who rebuilt the city after the great quake. ⓘ *30 min. Metro: Terreiro do Paço. Tram: 15, 25. Bus: 706, 711, 728, 735, 759, 774, 781, 782, 783.*

⑤ ★★ kids Elevador de Santa Justa. This striking iron structure towers over the Baixa. It was built in 1900 to haul weary pedestrians from the low-lying downtown up the hill to the chic Chiado district and is still in use, although fare hikes mean that these days it's used more by tourists seeking a one-off adventure than locals on their daily shopping run. Contrary to local lore, Gustave Eiffel had no role in its construction, although the ornate 148-foot iron frame certainly shares some style points with his Parisian tower. The views are great from the top, which you can

also reach by walking up the Rua do Carmo shopping street. ⓘ *10 min. Rua de Santa Justa. Return ticket 5.15€ . Winter daily 7am–9pm; summer daily 7am–11pm. Metro: Baixa-Chiado. Bus: 711, 736, 746, 759, 783.*

⑥ ★★★ kids Convento do Carmo & Museu Arqueológico. At the top end of the elevator stands a stark monument to nature's destructive power. The pointed Gothic arches of the Carmelite convent point eerily skyward like the ribs of a skeletal whale. The convent was built in the 14th century by Nuno Álvares Pereira, the kingdom's richest nobleman and a military hero for defeating Spanish invaders. When construction was completed, Álvares Pereira gave away his wealth and lived here as a humble monk; Pope Benedict made him a saint in 2009. Like most of Lisbon, the magnificent church tumbled in the 1755 earthquake, and its soaring nave was left as a roofless ruin. The surviving back rooms contain **archaeological exhibits,** including 6th-century Jewish gravestones, an Egyptian sarcophagus, and a pair of spooky Peruvian mummies. The main attraction, however, are the

The towering skeleton of Convento do Carmo, destroyed in the 1755 earthquake.

evocative ruins, particularly moving in the evening light. In the summer it hosts concerts, plays, and open-air movie screenings. ⏲ *1 hr. Largo do Carmo, 4. www.museuarqueologico docarmo.pt.* ☎ *21/346-0473. Admission 4€ adults, 3€ students & seniors; free 14 and under. May–Sept Mon–Sat 10am–7pm; Oct–Apr Mon–Sat 10am–6pm. Metro: Baixa-Chiado. Tram: 28. Bus: 758.*

6A **Café A Brasileira.** Lisbon's most famous cafe opened in 1905 serving coffee from Brazil. It's always been a favorite with writers and artists. Paintings from 1960s habitués decorate the interior, and a statue of poet Fernando Pessoa is seated on the terrace. Do like the locals do and take a shot of coffee and a sticky pastry standing at the long bar—prices are much cheaper there than at the tourist-filled outdoor tables. *Rua Garrett, 120.* ☎ *21/346-9541.*

7 ★★★ **kids** **Tram 28.** Once you've walked down from Carmo to the Chiado, a chic 19th-century shopping district, it's time to take the weight off your feet. From **Praça Luís de Camões,** jump on one of the little yellow streetcars clattering westward. Electric trams have been rattling around the city since 1901, and, after a long decline, old lines are being reopened. Running through the old heart of the city, No. 28 is always crowded with tourists, but it's a must-do. Take care with your belongings; the trams are a favorite hunting ground for pickpockets. ⏲ *30 min. 2.90€ single. Eastbound Mon–Fri 6:20am–11:25pm; Sat 6:20am–11:105pm; Sun 7:25am–11:10pm. Westbound Mon–Fri 5:40am–11:10pm; Sat 5:45am–10:30pm; Sun 6:45am–10:35pm. Services every few minutes.*

8 ★ **Basílica da Estrela.** Tram 28 stops directly outside this basilica, built in 1779 by Queen Maria I, who is entombed here. The two white bell towers and dome of this Lisbon landmark recall the baroque churches of Rome. A **nativity scene** containing more than 500 cork and terra-cotta figures by Portugal's greatest 18th-century sculptor Joaquim Machado de Castro is a main

Statue of poet Fernando Pessoa in front of Café a Brasileira.

attraction inside amid the Italian paintings and multicolored marble. In 1999 some 100,000 people packed the church and surrounding streets for the funeral of *fado* music diva Amália Rodrigues. Across the

Basílica da Estrela.

road the **Jardim da Estrela** is one of the city center's most relaxing parks, featuring water pools and shady tropical plants. ⏱ *20 min. Largo da Estrela.* ☎ *21/396-0915. Free admission. Daily 8:45am–8pm. Tram: 25, 28. Bus 713, 773, 774.*

❾ ★ Cemitério dos Prazeres. The end of the line for passengers on Tram 28 is the graveyard. Prazeres cemetery is Lisbon's largest, opened in the 1830s. It may seem like an unlikely attraction, but it's a fascinating place to visit, with lane after lane of cypress trees and ornate mausoleums built to house the remains of Portugal's grandest families. The **white pyramid** built in 1849 for the family of the Dukes of Palmela is Europe's largest private mausoleum. The cemetery lies on the edge of the leafy **Campo de Ourique** neighborhood, whose cafes, restaurants, and Art Deco buildings make this a pleasant place to stroll. ⏱ *30 min. Praça São João Bosco.* ☎ *21/3 96-1511. Free admission. Winter 9am–4:30pm; summer 9am–5:30pm. Tram: 25, 28. Bus 701, 709, 774.*

The Best in Two Days

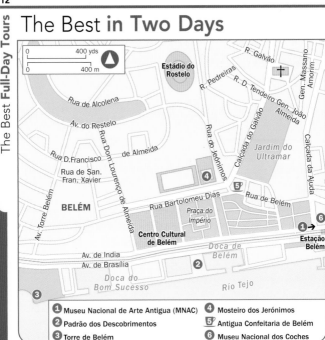

0 400 yds
0 400 m

Estádio do Rosteto

R. Galvão

R. Pedreiras

R. D. Tendeiro

Gen. João Almeida

Gen. Massano Amorim

Rua de Alcolena

Av. do Restelo

Rua de San. Fran. Xavier

Rua D.Francisco

Rua Dom Lourenço de Almeida

de Almeida

Rua do Jerónimos

Calçada do Galvão

Jardim do Ultramar

Calçada da Ajuda

BELÉM

Av. Torre Belém

Rua Bartolomeu Dias

Praça do Império

Rua de Belém

Centro Cultural de Belém

Doca de Belém

Estação Belém

Av. de India

Av. de Brasília

Doca do Bom Sucesso

Rio Tejo

❶ Museu Nacional de Arte Antigua (MNAC)
❷ Padrão dos Descobrimentos
❸ Torre de Belém
❹ Mosteiro dos Jerónimos
❺ Antigua Confeitaria de Belém
❻ Museu Nacional dos Coches

This tour takes you west along the Tagus to the historic riverside neighborhood of Belém and its monuments associated with Portugal's Age of Discovery. Start early to enjoy a couple of hours in Portugal's best-stocked art museum on your way to Belém. While the walk—4 miles from downtown—is doable, most will ride the bus, tram, or riverside commuter train. Bike hire is also becoming popular for the flat ride to Belém. START: **Museu Nacional de Arte Antigua. Bus: 713, 714, 727.**

❶ ★★★ **Museu Nacional de Arte Antigua (MNAC).** Portugal's greatest collection of Old Masters has the advantage of being housed in a clifftop 17th-century palace complete with a restaurant/cafe opening onto a grassy, sculpture-filled **garden** with jaw-dropping harbor views. As well as a world-class painting collection, the museum has rooms filled with goldware, ceramics, antique furniture, and textiles from around Europe and lands visited by Portuguese explorers. Masterpieces include the nightmarish *Temptations of St. Anthony* by Hieronymus Bosch, Francisco de Zurbarán's full-body portraits of the 12 Apostles, and a pair of golden 17th-century Japanese screens depicting Portuguese sailors arriving in Nagasaki. For many Portuguese, however, the museum's most-treasured item is the *Panels of St. Vincent,* a massive 1470s work by Nuno Gonçalves

The Age of Discovery

Starting in 1415, a small country, marginalized on the Western edge of Europe, managed to create the first global empire. The capture of the North African port of Ceuta in 1415 by a prince who would be known to history as Henry the Navigator started Portugal's Age of Discovery. Driven by religious zeal and hopes of riches, Portuguese sailors edged their wooden boats down the coast of Africa, across the Indian and Atlantic Oceans, and into the Pacific. In 1488 Bartolomeu Dias became the first European to reach the Cape of Good Hope. A decade later, Vasco da Gama found a sea route to India. Pedro Alvares Cabral landed in Brazil in 1500. Others founded trading posts in Japan, China, the spice islands of Indonesia, and the Persian Gulf. They opened up the world and for centuries made Lisbon a rich, cosmopolitan city. But there was an ugly side to the Age of Discovery. Portugal initiated the Atlantic slave trade, its ships delivering 6 million Africans into bondage. Colonial wars raged on into the 1970s by dictatorial rulers desperate to retain Lisbon's African empire.

depicting Lisbon society, from fishermen to royalty, at the time of the Discoveries. ⏱ *2 hr. Rua das Janelas Verdes.* ☎ *21/391-2800. www.museudearteantiga.pt. Admission 6€ adults; 3€ students and seniors; free 11 and under and disabled. Tues–Sun 10am–6pm. Bus: 713, 714, 727.*

❷ ★ **Padrão dos Descobrimentos.** The 50m-high Discoveries Monument was erected in the 1960s by Portugal's Fascist-inspired dictatorship to celebrate the Age of Discovery. It remains a striking landmark, jutting like the prow of a *caravela* sailing boat over the waters of the Tagus. From the bow to the stern, the pure white monolith is lined with outsized statues of Discoveries-era heroes from Henry the Navigator and Vasco da Gama to Gomes Eanes de Zurara, whose chronicles of Henry's exploits include a heart-rending description of a 1444 slave sale. Views from the top of the monument are impressive. ⏱ *30 min. Avenida de Brasília.* ☎ *21/303-1950.*

www.padraodosdescobrimentos.pt. Admission 5€ adults; 2.50€ seniors; free 11 and under. Oct–Feb 10am–7:30pm; Mar–Sept 10am–6:30pm.

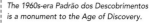

The 1960s-era Padrão dos Descobrimentos is a monument to the Age of Discovery.

Train: Belém. Tram: 15. Bus: 714, 727, 728, 729, 751.

❸ ★★ **kids** **Torre de Belém.** A walk along the Belém riverfront takes you to the most recognizable symbol of Lisbon: Belém Tower. This UNESCO World Heritage site is a prime example of the Manueline architecture, a uniquely Portuguese style named after a king who drove the discoveries and inspired by maritime motives. The graceful white tower looks more decorative than warlike, but it was built in the 16th century to defend the entrance to the Lisbon harbor and saw action in the 1830s when its cannons opened fire on French ships who intervened in Portugal's Civil War. The park surrounding it is a shaded place where you can contemplate the castellated tower and carvings of ropes, regal domes, shields, and intricate statues. The

The ornate side entrance to the Mosteiro dos Jerónimos.

inside can be a little underwhelming, especially if you've had to endure long lines to get in. ⓘ *30 min. Avenida de Brasília. www.torre belem.gov.pt* ☎ *21/362-0034. Admission 6€ ; 3€ seniors and students; free under 12. Oct–April Tues–Sun 10am–5pm; May–Sept Tues–Sun 10am–6pm. Train: Belém. Tram: 15. Bus: 714, 727, 728, 729, 751.*

❹ ★★★ **Mosteiro dos Jerónimos.** Like Belém Tower, this monastery was built on the orders of King Manuel I, in the 16th century. But where the interior of Belém Tower may underwhelm, this UNESCO World Heritage Site is a must-see. It's the city's most expressive showcase of the architectural style that takes Manuel's name, representing the newfound wealth and glory that came with Portugal's maritime expansion. The king paid for it with the so-called "pepper tax" on spices hauled from the East. Go early or late to avoid the longest lines.

Inside the 16th-century Mosteiro dos Jerónimos monastery.

Mosteiro dos Jerónimos

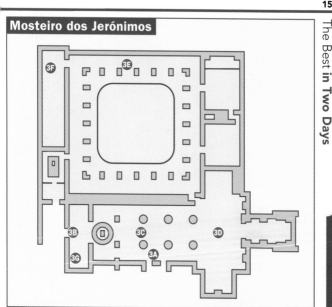

The **3A south portal** is the visual centerpiece of the exterior, an extraordinary shrine-like doorway carved with saintly figures and Portuguese heroes intertwined with the twisted ropes and exotic vegetation that characterizes the Manueline style. The **3B main portal,** built by French sculptor Nicolas Chantereine is more discreet but equally ornate, featuring figures of Manuel I and his queen Maria of Aragon.

The **3C three-aisled** interior is a showstopper. Slender columns like ship's masts bloom into flower-like supports for the web of tracery on the vaulted ceiling. It's a masterpiece by Spanish architect Juan de Castillo. Among the tombs of royalty and Portuguese notables, those of explorer Vasco da Gama (1460–1524) and poet Luis de Camões (1524–80) stand out. At the far end is the **3D capela-mor,** the

main chapel, built by Queen Catarina in 1571 with panels of Mannerist paintings.

Other highlights include the **3E cloisters** decorated with Manueline carvings and the **3F refectory** walls lined with 17th-century *azulejos* (tiles). Look out for the tomb of writer Fernando Pessoa (1888–1935) in the cloisters. In 1985, the leaders of Spain and Portugal signed the treaty taking their countries into the European Union upstairs in the cloisters. From the **3G choir,** you can take in the church from above and admire the carved stalls.

🕐 *1 hr. Praça do Império.* 📞 *21/362-0034. www.mosteirojeronimos. pt. Admission 10€ adults; 5€ seniors and students; free 11 and under. Oct–April Tues–Sun 10am–5pm; May–Sept Tues–Sun 10am–6pm. Train: Belém. Tram: 15. Bus: 714, 727, 728, 729, 751.*

Lining up for a pastes de Belém at the Antiga Confeitaria de Belém.

5 Antiga Confeitaria de Belém. This tile-covered cafe/bakery founded in 1837 is famed for the little custard tarts that have become one of Portugal's best-known culinary exports. Although they are known elsewhere as pasteis de nata, here they just call them pastes de Belém. Skip the lines for takeaway by grabbing a table in the waiter-service back room. You can always ask them to add a to-go box to your bill. *Rua de Belém, 84–92. www.pasteisde belem.pt.* ☎ *21/363-7423. $.*

6 ★★ kids Museu Nacional dos Coches. Release your inner Cinderella at one of the world's richest collections of horse-drawn cartridges. It's filled with lavishly decorated gilt coaches that once hauled royalty and aristocracy around the city. The oldest was used for the grand entry of King Filipe II into Lisbon in 1619. The golden coach shipped from Vienna by Emperor Joseph I for his sister's wedding is the most fairytale-like, but there's no evidence it was ever turned into a pumpkin.

Controversially, the museum was moved in 2015 into a ultramodern building across the road from its original home in the old royal stables. Still, it remains Portugal's most-visited museum. ⏱ *1 hr. Avenida da Índia n° 136. www.museudos coches.gov.pt.* ☎ *21/073-2319. Admission 10€. Tues–Sun 10am–5:30pm. Train: Belém. Tram: 15. Bus 714, 727, 729, 751.*

Gilded coaches in Lisbon's popular National Coach Museum.

The Best in Three Days

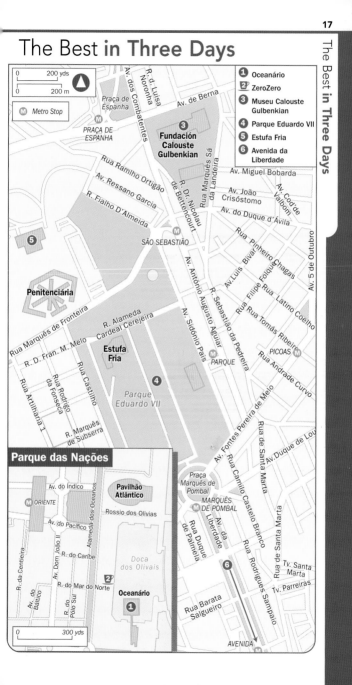

0   200 yds
0   200 m

Ⓜ Metro Stop

1 Oceanário
2 ZeroZero
3 Museu Calouste Gulbenkian
4 Parque Eduardo VII
5 Estufa Fria
6 Avenida da Liberdade

Praça de Espanha

Av. de Berna

R. d. Luísa Noronha

Av. dos Combatentes

PRAÇA DE ESPANHA

3 Fundación Calouste Gulbenkian

Rua Ramilho Ortigão

Av. Ressano Garcia

R. Fialho D'Almeida

R. Dr. Nicolau de Bettencourt

Rua Marquês Sá da Landeira

Av. Miguel Bobarda

Av. João Crisóstomo

Av. Cod de Valbom

Av. do Duque d'Ávila

SÃO SEBASTIÃO

Rua Pinheiro Chagas

Av. Luís Bivar

Rua Filipe Folque

Rua Latino Coelho

Av. 5 de Outubro

5

Penitenciária

Av. António Augusto Aguiar

R. Sebastião da Pedreira

Rua Tomás Ribeiro

PICOAS Ⓜ

Rua Marquês de Fronteira

R. Alameda Cardeal Cerejeira

Estufa Fria

Av. Sidónio Pais

PARQUE Ⓜ

Rua Andrade Curvo

R. D. Fran. M. Melo

Rua Castilho

Rua Rodrigo da Fonseca

4

Parque Eduardo VII

Av. Fontes Pereira de Melo

Rua de Santa Marta

Av. Duque de Lou

Rua Artilharia 1

R. Marquês de Subserra

Praça Marquês de Pombal

Rua Camilo Castelo Branco

Rua de Santa Marta

Parque das Nações

Av. do Índico

Pavilhão Atlântico

Ⓜ ORIENTE

Rossio dos Olivias

Av. do Pacífico

Alameda dos Oceanos

Av. Dom João II

R. do Caribe

Doca dos Olivais

MARQUÊS DE POMBAL Ⓜ

Rua Duque de Palmela

Av. da Liberdade

Rua Rodrigues Sampaio

Tv. Santa Marta

Tv. Parreiras

R. da Centieira

Av. do Báltico

R. do Pólo Sul

R. do Mar do Norte

2

Oceanário

1

6

Rua Barata Salgueiro

AVENIDA

0   300 yds

This tour explores the ancient city's more modern neighborhoods. We discover an extraordinary art collection amassed by a pioneer oil magnate, an aquatic wonderland, and Lisbon's most elegant shopping street. START: **Praça do Comércio. Metro Baixa-Chiado. Tram: 12, 15. Bus: 2, 81, 92, 711, 713.**

The gleaming waterfront Lisbon Oceanarium holds sharks, turtles, sea otters, and more.

1 ★★★ kids **Oceanário de Lisboa.** One of the world's most spectacular aquariums, the Oceanário opened as the centerpiece of the 1998 World's Fair. It remains a top attraction. At the core of the ultramodern riverside building is a 1.3-million-gallon tank, 23 feet deep and holding some 100 species including sharks, rays, barracuda, and a slow-moving ocean sunfish weighing in at over 1 ton. Floor-to-ceiling panels enable visitors to stay nose-to-nose with these creatures through their stay. Surrounding the main tank are four towers, representing life in the Atlantic, Indian, Antarctic, and Pacific oceans. Start your visit on the surface, ogling penguins, puffins, brilliantly colored frogs, and playful sea otters. Then spiral down through startlingly different ecosystems discovering psychedelically colored cuttlefish, jewel-like wrasse and puffers, shoals of luminous jellyfish. It's a delight for all ages, beautifully laid out and well explained. For a night to remember, book your kids for an overnight **sleepover party** next to the shark-filled tank. The oceanarium isn't cheap, but fees

support education and conservation work. It's located in the waterfront **Parque das Nações** district, which is packed with some startling architecture, including a huge shopping mall and a fun science center (p 44). ⏱ *2 hr. Esplanada Dom Carlos I.* ☎ *21/891-7000. www. oceanario.pt. Admission 15€ adults; 10€ seniors and kids 4–12; free 3 and under; 39€ families (2 adults/2 children under 13). Apr–Oct daily 10am–7pm; Nov–Mar daily 10am–6pm. Metro: Oriente. Bus: 26B, 728.*

The Volcano Fountain in the Parque das Nações.

Lisbon's Arts Philanthropist

Born in Istanbul to an Armenian merchant family, Calouste Sarkis Gulbenkian was one of the first to realize the potential of Middle East petroleum. He made a fortune in oil deals, earning the nickname "Mr. 5 Percent." He spent much of his money investing in art, from ancient artifacts to Impressionist masterworks. Amid the chaos of WWII, Gulbenkian settled in neutral Portugal, taking a room in a Lisbon hotel that remained his home until he died in 1955. He left much of his fortune, estimated at $840 million, to a Lisbon-based foundation to promote the arts, science, charity, and education. Today the Gulbenkian Foundation runs a museum housing his collection and organizes concerts, exhibitions, and research that play a central role in the cultural life of the city.

2 ★ **Zero-Zero.** This bright and cheerful pizza joint is a good bet for a quick post-Oceanarium lunch. It imports almost everything from Italy and bakes in wood-fired ovens. Pizzas range from 9€ for a margherita to 18.5€ for a topping of buffalo mozzarella and aged prosciutto di Parma. More than 80 Italian wines include house Prosecco on tap. *Alameda dos Oceanos, lote 2. www.pizzeria zerozero.pt.* ☎ *21/895-7 016. $$.*

The Calouste Gulbenkian foundation.

3 ★★★ **Museu Calouste Gulbenkian.** This is not the world's biggest art collection, but thanks to Gulbenkian's discerning taste, almost all the 6,000 items are masterpieces. The museum follows the path through the history of human creativity, from the funeral masks of ancient Egypt and Assyrian carvings from 888 B.C., to Greek vases and Roman jewelry, to Persian carpets, Ottoman ceramics, and Armenian bibles lavishly illustrated in the 1620s. There are galleries filled with rooms with furniture and tableware from the palaces of French kings and Russian czars. Rembrandts, Turners, and Manets shine among the European art. The final room is devoted to the gem-encrusted genius of Art Nouveau designer René Lalique. The entire collection is held in a low-lying 1960s building that also houses concert halls, conference rooms, and temporary exhibitions. Its landscaped **gardens,** filled with wild birds, leafy paths, and tumbling steams, are a perfect escape from the city bustle. On the other side of the gardens, a branch of the museum holds the foundation's excellent collection of **international and Portuguese modern art.** The same ticket gets you into both. You'll find good cafes/restaurants in both museums and in the gardens. *Avenida de Berna, 45A. www.gulbenkian.pt.* ☎ *21/782-3 461.*

The sprawl of Eduardo VII Park.

Admission 10€ adults 30 and over; 5€ seniors and ages 12–29; free 12 and under. Free for all Sun after 2pm. Wed–Mon 10am–6pm. Metro: São Sebastião, Praça de Espanha. Bus: 713, 716, 726, 742, 746, 756.

❹ ★★ Parque Eduardo VII. From the modern art museum, it's a short, but uphill walk to the top of central Lisbon's biggest green space. The view is worth the climb, an unimpeded panorama over the geometric hedge patterns running down the center of the park to the tree-lined Avenida da Liberdade shopping street and beyond to the river and the distant Arrábida mountains. The viewpoint is flanked by two pairs of laurel-wreath-topped columns typical of the imperial architecture favored by Portugal's 20th-century dictatorship and a smaller monument to the revolution that restored democracy in 1974. The country's biggest **Portuguese flag** also flaps from a 115-foot pole. Behind is the intimate **Jardim Amália Rodrigues,** named for the legendary *fado* singer who died in 1999. It features an outdoor cafe beside a cooling pond. The park has a popular book fair in July but looks best a month earlier when the jacaranda trees fill with purple blossom. *Parque, Marquês de Pombal. Bus: 713, 726, 742, 744, 746.*

❺ ★ Estufa Fria. On the western side of the park is a collection of hothouses filled with exotic vegetation. Amid streams and pools are coffee and mango trees, camellias, and cacti. It's a popular spot for locals to relax. *Parque Eduardo VII. www.estufa fria.cm-lisboa.pt. ☎ 21/8 17-0996. Admission 3.10€ adults; 1.55€ seniors and students; free 6 and under. Free for all Sun before 2pm. Apr–Oct daily 10am–6:30pm; Nov–Mar daily 9am–4:30pm. Metro: Parque. Bus: 713, 742.*

❻ ★★ Avenida da Liberdade. Lisbon's chicest shopping street since 1879 was inspired by Paris' Champs Elysées. It runs gently downhill for 1,200 yards from the Parque to the older Baixa district. Traffic roars up the central lanes, but pedestrians have pavements and two leafy boardwalks for strolling. There are grand old hotels like the Tivoli and Avenida Palace, theaters, banks, embassies, and vintage movie houses (now mostly closed, although the 1950s **Cinema São Jorge** still opens for festivals and special events). Mostly, though, the Avenida is for shopping.

Be on the lookout for distinctive Art Deco landmarks: the *Daily Planet*–like 1940 headquarters of the *Diário de Notícias* newspaper, earmarked for conversion into luxury apartments; the monumental Cineteatro Éden opened in 1937, now a hotel; and the headquarters of the Portuguese Communist Party. *Metro: Restauradores, Avenida, Marquês de Pombal. Bus: 709, 711, 732, 736, 746, 746, 783.* ●

The Best Special-Interest Tours

Food For Thought

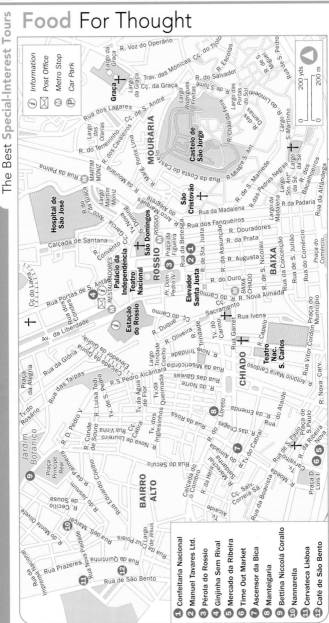

Information
Post Office
Metro Stop
Car Park

R. Voz do Operário
Largo da Graça
R. do Tijolo
Graça
Largo da Graça
Cç. da Graça
Trav. das Mónicas
Cc. do Tijolo
R. do Salvador
R. de S. Tomé
R. das Escolas
R. S. Pedro
Rua dos Lagares
Cç. de S. André
Rua dos Lagares
R. das Portas do Sol
Rue de S. Miguel
MOURARIA
Largo Rodrigues Freitas
R. da Costa do Castelo
Castelo de São Jorge
Rua de S. Mamede
Largo das Olarias
Cç. das Olarias
R. do Terreirinho
R. dos Cavaleiros
Ponte Nova
Largo da Graça
MARTIM MONIZ
R. Marquês Ponte Lima
R. da Mouraria
Arco do Marquês de Alegrete
São Cristovão
Rua da Madalena
R. de S. Mamede
R. de S. Ant.
R. das Pedras Negras
Largo da Sé
R. dos Bacalhoeiros
Rua da Alfândega
Hospital de São José
Rua da Palma
Calçada de Santana
R. da Graça
R. do Arco
T.ª Nova de S. Domingos
Convento
Palácio da Independência
São Domingos
ROSSIO
Praça da Figueira
Rua da Betesga
Rua dos Fanqueiros
R. Douradores
R. da Prata
R. de Sta. Justa
R. da Assunção
R. de S. Nicolau
Largo da Madalena
R. da Padaria
Teatro Nacional
Rua da Conceição
R. da Prata
R. de S. Julião
Praça do Comércio
RESTAURADORES
Rua Portas de S. Antão
Calçada do Lavra
Cç. do Lavra
Estação do Rossio
Pr. Dom Pedro IV
R. do Ouro
Elevador Santa Justa
BAIXA CHIADO
Rua do Comércio
Av. da Liberdade
Cç. do Carmo
R. Nova Almada
Praça do Município
Rua do Carmo
Praça do Município
R. Duque
Cç. do Sacramento
Rua Ivens
Praça da Alegria
R. da Glória
R. da Oliveira
R. Garrett
Teatro Nac. S. Carlos
Jardim Botânico
R. das Taipas
Elevador da Glória
Calçada da Glória
Largo Trindade Coelho
R.S. Pedro Alcântara
R. Nova Trindade
Rua da Misericórdia
CHIADO
R. Capelo
R. António Maria Cardoso
R. Vítor Cordon
Tv. do Rosário
R. D. Pedro V
R. Luísa Todi
Tv. da Queimada
R. da Atalaia
R. do Norte
R. das Gáveas
R. da Rosa
R. do Loreto
Praça Luís de Camões
R. Nova-Carv.
Largo de Jesus
R. da Boavista
R. D. Pedro V
R. Conde de Soure
R. da Vinha
Tv. dos Inglesinhos
R. da Emenda
BAIRRO ALTO
Praça Príncipe Real
Calçada do Combro
R. do Século
R. da Horta Seca
Rua da Boavista
Praça de S. Paulo
R. da Ribeira Nova
Praça D. Luís I
Jardim Botânico
R. do Jasmim
R. Cecílio de Sousa
R. Eduardo Coelho
R. do Monte Olivete
R. do Monte Olivete
R. Ant.ª de Aguiar
Rua da Quintinha
Rua das Praças
Rua de São Bento
Rua Nova da Piedade
Largo da Cruz Polais

200 yds
200 m

1 Confeitaria Nacional
2 Manuel Tavares Ltd.
3 Pérola do Rossio
4 Ginjinha Sem Rival
5 Mercado da Ribeira
6 Time Out Market
7 Ascensor da Bica
8 Manteigaria
9 Bettina Niccoló Corallo
10 Nannarella
11 Cerveteca Lisboa
12 Café de São Bento

The facade of Mude Museum of Fashion and Design in Rua Augusta with surfboards on the exterior.

Lisbon is a foodie's delight, from traditional markets gleaming with fresh fruit and shoals of seafood to centuries-old cafes and storied shops packed with hard-to-find delicacies. Food is deeply rooted in the country's national identity, and meeting over coffee or breaking bread at the lunch table are crucial social activities. As the country's gastronomic heart, Lisbon showcases the country's best, from paprika-laden sausages from the north to sticky Madeiran molasses cakes. Add excellent wines, great coffee, and a new wave of chefs giving a contemporary twist to classic traditions. This day-long walking tour gives you a taste of delicious Lisbon. START: Praça da Figueira. Metro: Rossio; Tram: 12, 15, 25.

❶ ★★★ Confeitaria Nacional.
One of Europe's oldest pastry shops is the place to sample a typical Portuguese breakfast: fresh fruit juice; a *meia-de-leite* (half espresso, half hot milk); and a *torrada* (a doorstop of butter-laden toast). Alternatively, try a croissant—the Portuguese adopted the French breakfast pastries but tend to fill them with ham and cheese. Largely unchanged since it was opened in 1829, this history-packed gem displays homemade pastries that would tempt the most calorie-conscious. Locals stand in line at Christmas time for its *bolo rei* (king of cakes), heavy with crystalized fruit. Eggy sponge cakes known as *austríacos* are the legacy of Austrian refugees who stayed here in WWII and left the recipe. Among the other cream- and chocolate-filled delights, the humble aniseed-flavored cake called *meia-lua* is many people's favorite. The National Confectionary also does savory snacks and lunch and sells its own brand of coffee. After you leave, take time to stroll around the square: **Praça da Figueira** is one Lisbon's most harmonious, surrounded by five-story buildings typical of the post-1755 earthquake Pombaline style and dominated by an equestrian statue of King João I. *Praça da Figueira, 18. www.confeitarianacional.com.* ☎ *21 342 4470. Coffee with milk 1.50€, toast 2€. Mon–Thurs 8am–8pm; Fri–Sat 8am–9pm; Sun 9am–9pm. Metro: Rossio; Tram: 12, 15, 25.*

❷ ★★ Manuel Tavares Lda.
Practically next door to the

Confeitaria Nacional.

Alluring Tipples: Portuguese *Vinho*

Only recently has the world woken up to the extraordinary variety of wines produced in sunny Portugal. For years, international interest in v*inho* was limited to cheap-and-cheerful rosés and the complex Porto and Madeira fortified wines. Now, the excellent reds and whites produced in the Douro, Alentejo, and other regions are globally renowned. Some are made on the edge of Lisbon's suburbs, like the sweet *Moscatel* dessert wines from just south of the Tagus. Fresh whites from the northern hillsides, known as *vinho verde*, make excellent partners for seafood. Port remains Portugal's most alluring tipple. It was invented in the age of sailing ships, when brandy was added to Douro wines to prevent spoiling during sea journeys. Wines produced on the volcanic island of Madeira are similarly fortified. America's founding fathers toasted their Declaration of Independence with Madeira wine.

Confeitaria is a grocery store founded in 1860. Manuel Tavares' shop is an Aladdin's cave for food lovers, with shelves stocked with Portuguese wines and liquors, hams hung from the ceiling, cabinets filled with pungent ewe's milk cheeses and smoky *chouriço* sausages, and jars of sticky preserved plums from the eastern city of Elvas (reportedly a favorite of Britain's Queen Elizabeth II). The staff takes pride in giving customers old-fashioned courtesy whether you're purchasing a paper bag of dried figs or heading to the basement for a vintage 1936 port at 3,990€ a bottle (rare wines are a specialty). *Rua da Betesga 1 A e B. www.manuel tavares.com.* ☎ *21/342-4209. Mon–Sat 9:30am–7:30pm Metro: Rossio. Tram: 12, 15, 25.*

❸ ★★ **Pérola do Rossio.** Portugal's colonial empire included Brazil, São Tomé, Timor, and other coffee-producing lands, so it's no surprise that this is a country of caffeine addicts. The "pearl of Rossio," in the same family since its opening in 1923, sells beans from all three countries and beyond as

well as a selection of fine teas (including from Portugal's Azores islands), cookies, preserves, and other local specialties. The neon sign is a landmark on downtown Rossio square. *Praça D. Pedro IV 105. www.peroladorossio.pt.* ☎ *21/342-0744. Mon–Sat 9:30am–1pm; 3pm–7pm. Metro: Rossio.*

❹ ★ **Ginjinha Sem Rival.** It might be a tad early for a drink, but since you're in the neighborhood, try a *ginjinha*. Hole-in-the-wall joints selling shots of this sweet cherry liqueur started springing up around Rossio square in the 1840s, and

Ginjinha Sem Rival.

several survive. "Without Rival" is among the most authentic. You take a glass "with" or "without" (actual cherries that soak in the bottle). Sip it quickly at the marble-topped bar and move on—feeling a little bit happier. *Rua Portas de Santo Antão 7.* ☎ *21/ 346-8231. Daily 8am–midnight. Metro Rossio.*

❺ ★★ Mercado da Ribeira. There's been a food market around here since the Middle Ages, but the great covered halls still in use today were built in the 1880s. The traditional side of the market has dazzling displays of cut flowers and rows of stalls laden with seasonal produce (cherries in June, oranges in winter). Side alleys have butchers' stalls with displays of offal and fishmongers offering everything from tiny clams to torpedo-size tuna. Supermarkets and gentrification may have robbed it some of its bygone bustle, but the Ribeira market remains a window onto the soul of the city. *Tip:* Avoid Mondays when there is no fresh fish catch and most stalls are closed. *Avenida 24 de Julho.* ☎ *21/346-2966. Mon–Sat 6am–2pm. Metro: Cais do Sodré; Tram: 15, 25. Bus: 706, 720, 728, 732, 738, 760.*

❻ ★★★ Time Out Market This western side of the Ribeira market hall is now one of Lisbon's most-visited attractions, a space filled with food outlets that's a treasure trove for gourmet travelers. You take your pick from the 40 or so restaurants, bars, and stores, and then grab one of the tables filling the vast central hall and tuck in. Food ranges from creative offerings by Michelin-starred chefs such as Henrique Sá Pessoa and Miguel Laffan to sushi, pizza, burgers, and Portuguese snacks like deep-fried cod cakes. There are stores to buy wine, cheese, or chocolate; a workshop space with themed cookery classes;

Mercado da Ribeira.

and late-night concerts and DJs. All of the outlets come with the seal of approval from the food critics at *Time Out* magazine, which opened the place in 2014, after the wholesale food market moved out. It can get a little manic at busy times, but it has brought new life to the area and become a must for visiting foodies. *Avenida 24 de Julho. www.timeout market.com.* ☎ *21/395-1274. Sun–Wed 10am–midnight; Thurs–Sat 10am–2am. Metro: Cais do Sodré; Tram: 15, 25. Bus: 706, 720, 728, 732, 738, 760. See p 122.*

❼ ★ Ascensor da Bica. Not a gastronomic attraction as such, but

The Time Out Market food hall.

after lunch at the market, you probably need a rest, so let this funicular rail car, installed in 1892, haul you uphill from behind the riverside market to the Chiado district. Of three such lines still operating, this is the most picturesque, running through the tightly packed lanes of the Bica neighborhood. The little yellow cars take about 5 minutes to deliver you uptown. *Rua de São Paulo, 232. 3.70€. Mon–Sat 7am–9pm; Sun 9am–9pm. Tram: 25; Bus 714, 774.*

8 ★★ **Manteigaria.** The *pastel de nata* is Lisbon's pastry of choice and has become one of Portugal's best-known culinary exports. The light and delicate version here may be the city's best, with a custard filling that's soft and creamy. Manteigaria makes so many *pastel de nata* that they always come out warm. Best with a shot of espresso (*uma bica*) and a sprinkling of cinnamon (*canela*). Watch the next tray being made in the open kitchen while you tuck in. *Rua do Loreto, 2. ☎ 21/347-1492. Daily 8am–midnight. Metro: Baixa-Chiado. Tram: 28.*

9 ★★ **Bettina Niccoló Corallo.** The family serving up Lisbon's best chocolate has roots in Italy, Portugal, and the tropical island of

The little yellow rail cars of Ascensor da Bica.

Pastel de nata from Manteigaria.

São Tomé, where they ran chocolate and coffee plantations. These days, their sinfully good slabs of darkest chocolate are sourced from Ghana, Venezuela, Bolivia, and the Dominican Republic. Add-ons include Calabrian oranges, Piedmont hazelnuts, or caramel salted Algarve salt. Enjoy coffee, hot chocolate, and a sorbet sitting amid the little store's plantation-chic decor. *Rua da Escola Politécnica 4. ☎ 21/386- 2158. Mon–Sat 11am–7pm. Tram: 24; Bus: 702; 758; 733.*

10 ★★★ **Nannarella.** The lines down the street on hot days are a signal that the *gelato* (ice cream) served here is especially divine. Constanza Ventura moved here from her native Rome and quickly established an army of fans. Using the best Italian techniques and natural ingredients, the little store offers 18 permanent flavors, two daily specials (Cassata Siciliana, many people's favorite, is on the menu on Thurs) and regular seasonal specials. Enjoy your cone in the gardens beside **Portugal's Parliament** building just down the hill. *Rua Nova da Piedade 64. www. nannarella.pt. ☎ 92-687-8553. Daily noon–10pm. Metro: Rato. Bus: 706, 727, 773.*

11 ★★ **Cerveteca Lisboa.** After a walk around the antique stores lining **Rua de São Bento,** it's time for a spot of refreshment to build

The Portuguese Parliament.

up an appetite for dinner. Portugal may be known for its wines, but this place on the beautiful **Praça das Flores** square showcases the country's emerging craft-beer scene. *Cerveja* produced by a dozen local breweries is available, as is a wide selection of suds from Belgium, Scandinavia, and beyond. *Praça das Flores 63. www.cervetecalisboa. com. No phone. Sun–Thurs 3:30pm– 1am; Fri–Sat 3:30–2am. Metro: Rato. Bus: 773.*

⓬ ★ **Café de São Bento.** Finish the day with a juicy steak at this clubby restaurant much favored by lawmakers from Parliament across the road. The decor is red velvet, wood paneling, and Victorian portraits. Fans say the beef is the best in town, and there's a fine list of Portuguese wines and liquors to wash it down. *Rua de São Bento, 212. www.en.cafesaobento.com.* ☎ *30-880-9285. Mon–Fri 12:30pm– 2:30pm; daily 7pm–2am. Metro: Rato. Bus: 706, 727, 773.*

Rue Sao Bento.

Child's Play: Lisbon with Kids

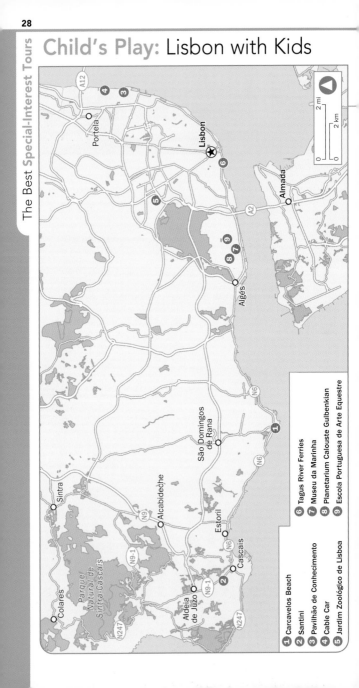

1 Carcavelos Beach
2 Santini
3 Pavilhão de Conhecimento
4 Cable Car
5 Jardim Zoológico de Lisboa
6 Tagus River Ferries
7 Museu da Marinha
8 Planetarium Calouste Gulbenkian
9 Escola Portuguesa de Arte Equestre

The magnificent display of aquatic life at the Oceanário de Lisboa is undoubtedly Lisbon's No. 1 attraction for kids (and many adults), but there's much else to keep children happy, from beach trips to a hands-on science museum, soccer superstar-themed hotel, and displays of dancing horses. START: **Carcavelos Beach. Train: Carcavelos.**

Carcavelos Beach.

❶ ★★ **Carcavelos Beach.** Lisbon is pretty much unique among European capitals in having long, warm summers and Atlantic surf rolling in onto sandy beaches in its suburbs. This broad expanse of sand at the mouth of the Tagus is a 25-minute train ride and 15-minute walk from downtown. Kids will be impressed by the mighty 16th-century fortress looming over the sand and the reliable but gentle waves that make this a perfect spot to learn to surf. Several certified **surf schools** (including www. carcavelossurfschool.com and www. angelsurfschool.com) offer classes to kids in English right here on the beach. Carcavelos has a number of restaurants and snack bars. Older youngsters may also be interested in the prestigious **Nova School of Business and Economics,** whose state-of-the-art campus opened in 2018 with a tunnel opening directly onto the beach. *Avenida Marginal, Carcavelos. Train: Carcavelos.*

❷ ★★ **Santini.** Close to Carcavelos station, this institution has delighted generations of Portuguese kids. Attilio Santini came from Italy to set up his first ice-cream shop on the Lisbon coast in 1949, serving thousands including the exiled royal families of Italy and Spain. It's still going strong. A standard set of flavors is always available (strawberry and cream is a classic mix), while seasonal favorites include Azores pineapple and sour cherry. Santini has several branches around Lisbon and along the coast. *Estrada da Torre.* www.santini.pt. ☎ 21/458-2374. *Daily 11am–midnight.*

The large central tank in Lisbon's popular Oceanário, in the Parque das Naçoes.

❸ ★★ **Pavilhão de Conheci-mento.** After a morning at the beach, head to the other end of town. Just a short walk from the Oceanário, in the ultramodern **Parque das Nações** district, the Knowledge Pavilion brims with the kind of interactive exhibits that lets kids have fun with science. Exhibitions change regularly but include stuff like suits that mimic conditions for astronauts walking on the moon; a bike you can ride on a tightrope high above the ground (a net and weights ensure that you don't fall off); foam blocks that allow budding architects to build arched Roman bridges that will hold their weight. It's educational and a bundle of laughs for youngsters and their parents. *Largo José Mariano Gago, 1. www.pav conhecimento.pt.* ☎ *21/891-7100. Admission 9€, 7€ youngsters 12–17, 6€ seniors & kids 3–11, free 2 and under; 24€ families (2 adults and with kids up to 17). Mon–Fri 10am–7:30pm, Sat–Sun 11am–6:30pm. Metro: Oriente. Bus: 728.*

❹ ★ **Cable Car.** Built, like the rest of the neighborhood, for the World's Fair of 1998, the cable car

Soccer superstar Cristiano Ronaldo exhibit in the Sporting Museum.

hauls you along over the riverbank, 100 feet up, offering spectacular views of the Tagus and the area's modern architectural landmarks such as the graceful **Vasco da Gama** bridge, Europe's longest at 7.6 miles, or the towering **Myriad Hotel,** once Lisbon's tallest building. The trip lasts about 10 minutes. *Passeio das Tágides. www.telecabine lisboa.pt.* ☎ *21/895-6143. One-way ticket 3.95€ adults; 2€ seniors and kids 7–12; free 6 and under. Spring and fall 11am–7pm; summer 10:30am–8pm; winter 11am–6pm. Metro: Oriente. Bus: 728.*

❺ ★★ **Jardim Zoológico de Lisboa.** Lisbon Zoo has been around for 132 years and is home to more than 2,000 animals from 300 different species. At least one you're unlikely to see anywhere else: The Iberian lynx is the world's rarest cat, struggling for survival with the help of a conservation program in the wildlands of southern Spain and southeastern Portugal. The zoo has turned itself around after falling on hard times during the 1980s and is now a much-loved attraction for Portuguese schoolchildren who come to see the rare red pandas, dolphin show, or the "enchanted woods" where exotic birds fly in the open air. It's designed to get you as close as possible to the animals and includes a cable car that whisks visitors over the enclosures. *Praça*

The Myriad Hotel.

Where's Ronaldo?

For soccer-crazy kids, a trip to Portugal is a chance to get close to its most famous son, Cristiano Ronaldo. You could take the 2-hour flight from Lisbon to the island of Madeira, where the soccer superstar was born in 1985, to see the infamous statues and the museum containing his bazillion trophies (arriving at Madeira's aptly named **Cristiano Ronaldo International Airport**). But you can also find traces of the soccer superstar right here in Lisbon. The **Sporting Clube de Portugal** is where CR7 began his professional career, and memorabilia of the teenage prodigy is exhibited at the club's **sporting museum** (Rua Professor Fernando da Fonseca; www.sporting.pt; ☎ 21/751-6164; admission 14€ adults, 7€ children 6–13 and seniors, free for 5 and under; Metro: Campo Grande). To get an even more personal take on the Ronaldo lifestyle, check in to the **Pestana CR7 Hotel,** partly owned by the star. This downtown hotel is packed with high-tech gadgetry, soccer-themed decor, and screens showing the man in action. The colorful rooms and hip bar are aimed more at an adult clientele, but children who love Ronaldo will probably love his hotel too (Rua do Comércio 54; www.pestanacr7.com; ☎ 21/040-1710; double 116€–373€; Metro: Terreiro do Paço; Tram 15, 25; see map p 144).

Marechal Humberto Delgado www.zoo.pt. ☎ 21/723-2900. Admission 21.50€ adults; 160€ seniors, 14.50€ kids 3–12; free 2 and under. Daily summer 10am–6:45pm; winter 10am–5:15pm. Metro: Jardim Zoológico. Bus: 701, 716, 726, 731, 746, 754, 755, 758, 768, 770.

⑥ ★★ Tagus River Boat Trip. There are a growing number of ways to take to the water in Lisbon. **HIPPOtrip** (www.hippotrip.com) runs amphibious buses that tour sites on land before rolling into the water to chug past the Belém waterfront. Others offer trips by

Entrance to Lisbon's Zoo.

Explore the city from the Tagus River via HIPPOtrip's amphibious buses.

motorboats and sailing yachts (www.lisbonbyboat.com), or on brightly painted historic boats that once carried cargo between the shores (www.nossotejo.pt). A cheaper option is to cross the Tagus on one of the ferries that take thousands of commuters to and from work every day. Fast catamarans zip across to the south bank towns of Montijo or Seixal, but the shortest and most frequent route is on the little orange boats that take 10 minutes to run from Cais do Sodré station to the lively quayside neighborhood of Cacilhas. There, the nautically minded can tour the gundecks of a 19th-century warship **Dom Fernando II** (www.ccm. marinha.pt) in the **Museu da Marinha** (see below). *www.transtejo. pt.* ☎ *80-820-3050. Metro/bus passes can be used on the river ferries. Single tickets on the Lisbon-Cacilhas 1.25€; Lisbon-Montijo 2.75€. Weekday sailings to Cacilhas 5:35am–1:40am.*

❼ ★★ Museu da Marinha. The warship *Dom Fernando II* is operated by this Naval Museum based in the Belém district in an annex of the **Jerónimos Monastery** (p 14). It's backed with artifacts from Portugal's maritime history with a focus on the Discoveries. Highlights include the gilded **Royal Barge,** built in 1780 and last used to carry Britain's Queen Elizabeth II on a 1950s visit; the seaplane flown to

Brazil in 1922 on the first aerial crossing of the South Atlantic; and a wooden statue carried by Vasco da Gama on his first voyage to India. *Praça do Império. www.ccm. marinha.pt.* ☎ *21/097-7388. Admission 6.50€ adults; 3.25€ kids 4–12 and seniors;, free for 3 and under. Oct–Apr daily 10am–4:30pm; May–Sept daily 10am–5:30pm. Train: Belém. Tram: 15. Bus: 714, 727, 28, 729, 751.*

❽ ★ Planetarium Calouste Gulbenkian. Star-struck youngsters can lie back and gaze at the cosmos in the Planetarium, which is linked to the next-door Naval Museum. The central dome presents more than 9,000 stars in the

The stately Navy Museum.

Shoppers in the Colombo Centre.

9:30am–noon and 1:30pm–4pm; Sat 1:30–4pm.Train: Belém. Tram: 15. Bus: 714, 727, 28, 729, 751

9 ★ **Escola Portuguesa de Arte Equestre.** Horse lovers will delight in the dressage skills per-formed regularly by the Portuguese School of Equestrian Art in a spe-cially designed riding ring just up the road from Belém's **National Coach Museum** (p 16). Wearing 18th-century aristocratic garb, the team executes a series of near-perfect routines mounted on beau-tiful **Lusitano horses,** in efforts to maintain the ancient tradition of Portuguese riding skills. Visitor can watch hour-long training sessions Tuesday through Saturday at 10am, or attend grand gala nights held the final Friday of each month at 9:30pm. Check in advance for other times. *Calçada da Ajuda, next to No. 23. www.arteequestre.pt.* ☎ *21/923-7300. Training sessions 8€–12€; gala nights 25€–37.50€. Tram: 15. Bus: 728, 714, 727, 729, 751.*

night sky in a spectacular display of celestial light. Check in advance to see when sessions in English are offered. *Praça do Império. www.ccm. marinha.pt.* ☎ *21/097-7388. Admis-sion 5€, 2.50€ kids 4–12, over 65s, free for under 4s. Tues–Fri and Sun*

Soccer & Shopping

There are two big reasons for families to head out to the Ben-fica district: soccer and shopping. **Benfica** is Portugal's biggest soccer club (despite the efforts of crosstown rival **Sporting;** p 130). Nicknamed "the Eagles," Benfica has twice been European cham-pion and is a five-time runner-up. It claims 14 million supporters worldwide. If you can't catch a Benfica game at the 65,000-seat **Estádio da Luz** (Stadium of Light), check out the high-tech stadium museum, packed with interactive exhibits, many devoted to the club's greatest player, **Eusebio** (1944-2014) *(Av. Eusébio da Silva Ferreira; www.museubenfica.slbenfica.pt.;* ☎ *21/721/950; admis-sion: 10€ adults, 6€ seniors, 4€ children 3–14, free for 2 and under [stadium tour extra]; daily 10am–6pm (closed during matches); Metro: Alto dos Moinhos; Bus 750, 754, 768).*

Next door to the stadium is one of Europe's biggest shopping malls. The **Colombo Centre** *(Avenida Lusíada; www.colombo.pt.;* ☎ *21/711-3600; daily 9am–midnight; Metro: Colégio Militar/Luz; bus: 750, 799, 767)* contains 340 stores, 60 restaurants, 9 cinema screens, and a bowling alley. It's a useful rainy-day refuge.

True Romance

| 0 | 200 yds |
| 0 | 200 m |

Rua Rosa Araújo
Rua Barata Salgueiro
Tv. Parreiras
Rua Castilho
Rua do Salitre
AVENIDA
Jardim Botânico
Rua do Passadiço
Rua do Cardal
Rua de S. José
Av. da Liberdade
Tv. do Salitre
Praça da Alegria
Rua de Sa. Fé
R. S. António Capuchos
R.M. Bento Sousa
R. Instituto Bacteriológico
R. do Saco
R. Antero de Quental
solos sop ʌ
R. Maria Andrade
Praça Príncipe Real
Tv. do Rosário
Rua da Glória
Rua das Taipas
R. D. Pedro V
PCç do Lavra
Rua Portas de S. Antão
Calçada de Santana
Hospital de São José
R. do Desterro
R. da Palma
Rua do Benformoso
Rua das Olarias
GRAÇA
Tv. da Hora
R. Luísa Todi
Tv. de S. Pedro
R.S.Pedro Alcântara
Elevador da Glória
RESTAURADORES
MARTIM MONIZ
Largo Martim Moniz
R. do Terreirinho
Rua dos Lagares
Graça
BAIRRO ALTO
Tv. dos Inglesinhos
Estação do Rossio
Teatro Nacional
São Domingos
Cç. Garcia
R. da Mouraria
R. Marg. Ponte Lima
MOURARIA
R. da Rosa
Rua da Atalaia
Rua da Barroca
R. do Norte
R.da Horta Seca
R.C. Trindade
Tv. do Carmo
R. do Carmo
Cç. do Carmo
ROSSIO
ROSSIO
Pr. Dom Pedro IV
Rua da Betesga
R. de Sta. Justa
Rua da Madalena
Rua dos Fanqueiros
Rua dos Correeiros
R. da Prata
Rua da Costa do Castelo
Castelo de São Jorge
R. das Damas
CHIADO
R. da Hera
R. do Loreto
Rua das Flores
Rua do Alecrim
R. António Maria Cardoso
Rua Garret
Rua Ivens
Rua Nova Almada
BAIXA-CHIADO
BAIXA
R. dos Douradores
R. de S. Mamede
Sé
R.da Padaria
R. do Barão
ALFAMA
R. Moeda
R. da Bica
R. do Carvalho
Praça de S.Paulo
Rua Vitor Cordón
Rua da Conceição
Rua de S. Julião
Rua do Comércio
R. dos Bacalhoeiros
Praça D. Luís I
Teatro Nac. S. Carlos
R. Nova Carv.
Praça do Município
Rua da Alfândega
CAIS DO SODRÉ
Estação Cais do Sodré
Cais do Sodré
Av. Ribeira das Naus
Rua do Arsenal
Praça do Comércio
TERREIRO DO PAÇO
Av. Infante Dom Henrique
Doca de Marinha
Estação Fluvial Terreiro do Paço

Río Tejo

❶ Miradouro de Sophia de Mello Breyner Andresen
❷ Sunset River Cruise
❸ Chapitô à Mesa
❹ Memmo Alfama Hotel
❺ BSPA by Karin Herzog (spa)
❻ Quinta da Regaleira
❼ Carriage Ride to Palacio da Pena
❽ Tivoli Palace de Seteais Hotel
❾ Cabo da Roca
❿ Nortada

i	Information
✉	Post Office
Ⓜ	Metro Stop
Ⓟ	Car Park

Narrow lanes lit with yellow street lamps, the soft sound of fado music, endless riverside walkways: Lisbon oozes romance. Our weekend tour takes in some of the city's best spots for lovers—with a detour out to a lonely beach and the hilltop suburb that calls itself the capital of romance. START: **Miradouro de Sophia de Mello Breyner Andresen. Tram: 28. Bus: 734.**

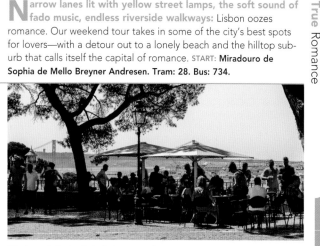

Miradouro de Sophia de Mello Breyner Andresen.

① ★★ Miradouro de Sophia de Mello Breyner Andresen.

You'll have the whole city at your feet when you visit this hilltop viewpoint. It has one of the city's most stunning views, from the gardens of São Jorge to the distant river and the tangle of narrow lanes of the medieval Mouraria district below. More commonly known as Miradouro da Graça after the handsome baroque church that overlooks the space, it was officially named after poet Sophia de Mello Breyner Andresen (1919–2004). There's more

Sunset river cruise.

poetry at the cute little bar just behind the church. Long a hotbed of intellectual fervor, **O Botequim** (Largo Graça 79) was opened in 1968 by poet and politician Natália Correia (1923–1993), whose erotically charged verses challenged ideas of sexuality during the long years of ultraconservative dictatorship. After enjoying the view, take a stroll through the winding alleys of **Alfama** (p 46). *Miradouro de Sophia de Mello Breyner Andresen, Calçada da Graça. Tram: 28. Bus: 734.*

② ★★ Sunset River Cruise.

The best way to see Lisbon is from the water, and sunset is the most romantic time. Choose from a wide range of options, from a couple of hours on a yacht (www.palma yachts.com) starting at around 30€, to a cruise on a party boat with DJ sets and a bar running into the night (www.veltagus.com). If that sounds too raucous for your romantic evening, you could charter your own boat—from a rigid inflatable to a sailing yacht—just for the two of you (www.lisbonbyboat.com).

The Street of Flowers

Rua das Flores (Street of Flowers) descends steeply from chic Chiado to the Cais do Sodré. It's lined with grand 18th-century buildings and holds a teaming market, hot nightlife, and a riverside pathway. At the top end is a palm-filled square fronted by the **Palácio Chiado,** built in 1777 by a party-loving aristocrat. It's sumptuously restored and filled with restaurants and bars (*Rua do Alecrim, 70; www.palaciochiado.pt; ☎ 21/010-1184; Sun–Thurs noon–midnight, Fri–Sat noon–2pm*). If romance needs chocolate, **Landeau** is the place. The snug, cellar-like cafe serves just one thing to eat: a chocolate cake so intensely flavored that the *New York Times* called it "devilishly good" (*Rua das Flores, 70; www. landeau.pt; ☎ 91-181-0801; daily noon–7pm*). A couple of doors down, the stylish bar **By the Wine** has a unique curved ceiling covered with back-lit bottles. It's run by the José Maria da Fonseca winery and serves a wide selection of wines. Romantics might want to try one of the strong, sweet *moscatels,* a specialty from the region just south of Lisbon. Among the food, cured *Ibérico* ham stands out (*Rua das Flores 41-43; www.bythewine.pt; ☎ 21/342-0319; Sept–June Tues–Sun noon–midnight, Mon 6pm–midnight; July–Aug daily 6pm–midnight*).

3 **Chapitô à Mesa.** It may seem odd, but Lisbon's circus school runs one of the city's most romantic restaurants. There are no clowns or jugglers, just amazing views over the city and a special atmosphere. Simple food is served in the leafy courtyard bar, but the real treat is upstairs where window seats look out over the vista and the chef serves his delicious modern take on Portuguese cuisine. Book ahead. *Rua Costa do Castelo 7. ☎ 21/888-0154. $$–$$$*

4 ★★★ **Memmo Alfama Hotel.** The boutique hotel in the heart of Lisbon's most charming neighborhood offers the best sun-rise views in Lisbon. Watch as dawn turns the vast expanse of the Tagus a shimmering gold—you'll see why locals call it the "sea of straw." The pool, breakfast terrace, and most rooms also have tremendous views over the red rooftops of Alfama and the towers and domes of its churches. Standard rooms are not huge but have a Scandinavian sleekness, and you can shell out for an upgrade and get your own personal terrace. There are a couple of intimate, brick-vaulted alcoves for a final nightcap, if you've had enough of looking at views. *Travessa das Merceeiras, 27. www.memmohotels. com. ☎ 21/049-5660. 42 units. Doubles 138€–380€. Tram 28. Bus 737. Map p 134.*

5 ★★ **BSPA by Karin Herzog.** It's time for some pampering. After a morning stroll along the **Belém waterfront** (p 66), head to the striking white oblong that is the **Altis Belém Hotel.** The spa here is on two levels. In the gently lit basement there are saunas, hammams, a

The 90-foot-deep "initiation well" at the Quinta da Regaleira palace.

broad marble pool, and a vast range of massages and body therapies using Swiss skincare techniques. It's all very zen. What truly sets it apart from its rivals, however, is upstairs, where a rooftop pool and sundeck reside right on the quayside. *Doca do Bom Sucesso. www.altishotels. com.* ☎ *21/040-0200. 55-min. "Be In Love" massage for couples 160€. Reservations required. Train: Belém. Tram: 15. Bus 729. Map p 133.*

⑥ ★★ **Quinta da Regaleira.** We've come out to Sintra, a 40-minute train or car ride from downtown Lisbon. Built amid a thickly forested mini mountain range between Lisbon and the Atlantic, the town has been a getaway for the upper crust since medieval times. The hills are peppered with palaces, none dreamier than this eccentric pile built in 1910 by a mystical millionaire. The palace is a gothic fantasy of towers, spires, and gargoyles filled with mysterious symbols linked to alchemy, magic, and secret societies. It's surrounded by lush tropical gardens where paths uncover dramatic statues, grottoes, and fountains. Oddest of all is the so-called "initiation well," a 90-foot pit with a staircase spiraling down into the bowels of the earth. *Rua Barbosa do Bocage, 5, Sintra. www.regaleira. pt.* ☎ *21/910-6650. Admission 6€ adults; 4€ ages 6-17 and seniors; free for 5 and under and 80 and over. Apr–Sept daily 9:30am–7pm; Oct– Mar daily 9:30am–5pm. Train: Sintra.*

⑦ **Carriage Ride to a Fairy-tale Castle.** This may be romantic overkill, but it's a delight anyway. Hire a horse and carriage to whisk you through the forest to the spectacular **Palácio da Pena** (p 163), the mountaintop former summer home of Portugal's royal family. You can hop on the carriage that regularly makes the 20-minute ride for 3.50€ or get an exclusive 1-hour ride for 75€ from the palace administrators (www.parques desintra.pt). Private operators also offer a 3-hour roundtrip for 110€ and a series of other rides to see more of Sintra's UNESCO World Heritage charm. (www.sintratur.com).

⑧ ★★★ **Tivoli Palacio de Seteais Hotel.** Stop for the night in an elegant mansion built for the Dutch ambassador in 1787. Lord Byron apparently composed poems in the gardens. Later guests have included Agatha Christie and Brad Pitt (not together). It is one of the

Dining in the Nobel Hall in the Tivoli Palacio de Seteais Hotel.

finest places to stay in Portugal: The rooms and salons are delightfully opulent, and views across the hills are exquisite. Complete your romantic day with dinner in the hotel restaurant surrounded by dainty nature paintings and sipping on the local Colares wine. *Rua Bar-*

Bardot and Baixa Views

When it opened in 1958, the **Hotel Mundial** was the place, hosting the likes of Roger Moore, Alain Delon, and Brigitte Bardot. These days, its panoramic top-floor restaurant, **Varanda de Lisboa,** is rather unfashionable, popular with business types for its "executive lunch" or older couples at weekends. That should change, because its cooking is excellent, the service immaculate, and the breathtaking views over the Baixa among the city's best. Sample one of its tableside flambés for a real touch of timeless romance. In addition to classic Portuguese and some French dishes, there are regular seasonal specials. Come in fall for venison and hare, or February for shad or lamprey. *Praça Martim Moniz 2. www.hotel-mundial. pt.* ☎ *21/884-2000. Main courses 18€–32€. Open daily. Metro: Martim Moniz (map p 98).*

Tableside flambé at Varanda.

Praia Grande beach.

bosa du Bocage, 8, Sintra. www.tivoli hotels.com. ☎ 21/9 233 200. 30 units. Doubles 344€–474€. Train: Sintra.

9 ★★★ Cabo da Roca For the final morning of your romantic tour, head to the most westerly point of the Eurasian land mass. This dramatic spot is where the Sintra mountains meet the Atlantic in a series of soaring cliffs. A plaque reads "Where the land ends and the sea begins," the words of Portugal's great 16th-century seafaring poet, Luís de Camões. A lighthouse stands 500 feet above the waves. Walks along the clifftops can be bracing in the often-blustery winds; be sure to stay within the safety rails. Renting a car makes it easier to discover the wild western coast, but a bus running between Cascais and Sintra stops at this remote spot. Estrada do Cabo da Roca. ☎ 21/928-0081 (tourist office). Bus: 403. Map p 154.

10 Nortada ★★★. End your romantic tour by soaking up some rays on one of the many sandy beaches tucked between the cliffs here. Praia Grande gets the nod, not least for the marvelous clifftop restaurant perched above the beach, specializing in seafood plucked fresh from the ocean below. The chargrilled fish and rice with lobster, shrimp, and clams are as mouthwatering as the views. If you're not driving, try a glass of Casal Santa Maria white wine, produced just up the road in Europe's most westerly vineyard. Avenida Alfredo Coelho 8, Praia Grande, Colares. www.restaurantenortada. com. ☎ 21/929-1516. $$–$$$.

Monument and lighthouse at Cabo da Roca.

Modern Moves

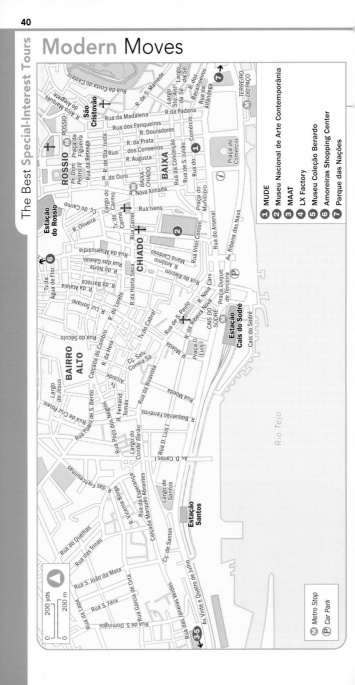

1 MUDE
2 Museu Nacional de Arte Contemporânia
3 MAAT
4 LX Factory
5 Museu Coleção Berardo
6 Amoreiras Shopping Center
7 Parque das Nações

Ⓜ Metro Stop
Ⓟ Car Park

Lisbon is revered for its old-world charm, but this tour takes you to its artistically modern side. We'll soak up some of its contemporary art collections and cutting-edge architecture and take a closer look at the city's renowned street-art scene. START: **MUDE. Rua Augusta, 24. Tram: 28. Bus 714, 732, 736, 746, 766, 783.**

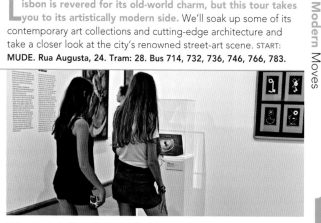

Visitors inside the Museu Nacional de Arte Contemporânea.

❶ ★★ MUDE. The name means "change" in Portuguese. It stands for **Museu do Design e da Moda** (Fashion and Design Musem), and it occupies the six-story former head-quarters of the bank that once financed the colonial empire (hence the politically incorrect mosaic in the lobby). A major overhaul was underway at press time, but the museum is scheduled to reopen in 2019. The "raw" design that helped make it one of Lisbon's most popular museums is set to stay, leaving much of the bank's interior stripped to bare concrete with derelict-chic remnants of its 1960s heyday. The permanent collection will return, featuring fashion and design icons from the 20th and 21st centuries. Space is being increased for temporary shows, stores, workshops, cafes, and restaurants. One thing that will remain unchanged are the bank's basement strong rooms, its most atmospheric exhibition space. *Rua Augusta, 24. www.mude.pt.* ☎ *21/817-1892. Free admission. Tues–Thurs and Sun 10am–8pm; Fri–Sat 10am–10pm. Metro: Baixa Chiado. Tram: 28. Bus 714, 732, 736, 746, 766, 783.*

❷ ★★ Museu Nacional de Arte Contemporânea. It's known popularly as the MNAC or Museu do Chiado, after the neighborhood. The official title is a little misleading, because in addition to contemporary artists, the collection presents a panorama of Portuguese art from the mid-19th century. Names to look out for include Almada Negreiros, Amadeo de Souza-Cardoso, Columbano Bordalo Pinheiro, José Malhoa, and Paula Rego. The museum is housed in a sprawling building that was once a convent and then a cookie factory. Renovation in the 1990s transformed the space, giving it an impressive sculpture filled-atrium and tables in the garden for the pleasant cafe. Despite a recent expansion into a neighboring building, there's not enough space to display all 5,000 works, so the collection is regularly rotated. *Rua Serpa Pinto 4. www.museuarte contemporanea.gov.pt.* ☎ *21/343-2148. Admission 4.50€ adults, 2.25€ students and seniors, free for children 12 and under. Tues–Sun 10am–5.30pm. Metro: Baixa-Chiado. Tram: 28.*

Lisbon as Canvas

Lisbon has emerged as one of Europe's most vibrant hubs for street art. Amid the mindless graffiti daubed on churches, historic monuments, trains, businesses, and private homes are dozens of striking murals that have earned Lisbon a reputation as one of the top cities for street art. You can see some of the best-known spots by organized tour (www.livingtours.com) or take a self-guided tour using a map of leading works (www.stick2target.com). Or just keep your eyes open as you wander the city. Among the most arresting works are the portrait of *fado* legend Amália Rodriques by **Vhils** at Calçada do Menino de Deus, 1-3 in Alfama; the house-sized *Racoon* created by **Bordallo II** out of auto parts near Rua Bartolomeu Dias, 43, just behind Belém Cultural Center; the tribute to Portugal's 1974 democratic revolution by U.S. artist **Shepard Fairey** at Rua Natália Correia 11; and the murals by an international group of artists covering a whole block of abandoned buildings halfway down **Avenida Fontes Pereira de Melo.** Off the beaten track but well worth a visit is **Quinta do Mocho,** a gritty immigrant neighborhood on the far side of Lisbon airport where tenement blocks are decorated with almost 70 murals in what's believed to be Europe's biggest urban art space. Tours of Quinto do Mocho can be arranged at facebook.com/GuiasdoMocho.

❸ ★★★ MAAT. The latest spectacular addition to the Lisbon art scene, the **Museum of Art, Architecture and Technology** opened in 2016. Designed by British architect Amanda Levete, the building rises like a soft white wave over the Tagus, revolutionizing Lisbon's riverfront. It connects and contrasts with the early-20th-century power plant next door, among whose giant turbines exhibitions are also held. The MAAT showcases the art collection of the EDP power company and hosts regular temporary exhibitions by Portuguese and international artists. Even those with little stomach for contemporary art will enjoy

The riverfront MAAT museum and Lisbon's 25th April Bridge, Europe's longest suspension span.

Urban graffiti in the LX Factory.

strolling on the roof and taking in the views. *Avenida de Brasília, Central Tejo. www.maat.pt.* ☎ *21/002-8130. Admission 5€ adults, 2.50€ students and seniors; free for ages 18 and under and the unemployed (general free admission first Sun of the month). Combined ticked with the Central Tejo power plant 9€. Wed–Mon 11am–7pm. Train: Belém. Tram: 15. Bus: 728, 714, 727, 729, 751.*

❹ ★★★ **LX Factory.** In the shadow of the April 25 Bridge, this rambling postindustrial area has become Lisbon's hippest place to work, shop, and hang out. This former textile factory and printworks was transformed into studios, offices, design and book stores, and cool restaurants and cafes. You can get a massage, knock down a glass of Mezcal, or buy designer shoes made from cork (Portugal is the world's biggest producer) without moving more than a few yards. Striking artworks are scattered around, and an open-air food and handicraft market is held on Sunday mornings. *Rua Rodrigues de Faria, 103. www.lxfactory.com.* ☎ *21/314-3399. Free admission. Daily 6am–2am (individual retailers have their own hours; for example, the Ler Devagar bookshop normally opens at noon). Train: Alcantara-Mar. Tram 15,18. Bus: 714, 720, 727, 732, 738, 751.*

❺ ★★★ **Museu Coleção Berardo.** In the depths of the bunker-like **Centro Cultural de Belém** (CCB) is a ground-breaking collection of modern and contemporary art. It was assembled by Joe Berardo, an emigrant from Madeira Island who made a fortune in South Africa. The museum covers the greats of 20th-century art including Jackson Pollack, Roy Liechtenstein, and Giorgio de Chirico, along with cutting-edge contemporary artists. Opened in 1992 across from Jerónimos Monastery, the CCB is itself a modern architectural landmark. It's Portugal's biggest cultural space and has a packed program of concerts, plays, and other events (p 127). *Praça do Imperio. www.en.museuberardo.pt.* ☎ *21/361-2878. Admission 5€ adults; 2.50€ students, seniors, and ages 7–18; free for children 6 and under (also free general admission Sat). Daily 10am–6.30pm. Train: Belém. Tram: 15. Bus: 714, 727, 728, 729, 751.*

❻ ★★★ **Amoreiras Shopping Center.** When they were built in the 1980s, the multicolored postmodernist towers of this mall were seen as a symbol of Portugal's emergence as a modern European

Cutting-edge artwork in the Centro Cultural de Belém.

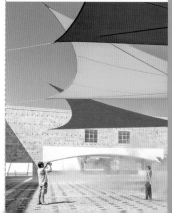

The gleaming Amoreiras Shopping Center, Lisbon's oldest shopping mall.

state after decades of dictatorship and years of revolutionary turmoil. The ritzy retail center was also a symbol of rampant consumerism, but it's stood the test of time and remains both architectural landmark and one of the chicest places in the country to shop (p 80). The rooftop viewing platform is the city's highest spot. *Av. Eng. Duarte Pacheco. www.amoreiras.com.* ☎ *21/381-0200. Rooftop viewing point:*

Admission 5€ adults; 3€ seniors and children 6–12; free for children 5 and under. Check site for timings. Daily 10am–11pm. Metro: Rato, Marquês de Pombal. Bus: 713, 758, 774.

❼ ★★ Parque das Nações. Built for the Expo98 World Fair. This riverside neighborhood is a showcase for modern Lisbon. Architectural landmarks include the **Estação do Oriente,** an airy-white railway station designed by the Spanish architect Santiago Calatrava, and the **Pavilhão de Portugal**, the brainchild of Portugal's own architectural superstar Álvaro Siza Vieira. The **Vasco da Gama bridge** is Europe's longest, and the **Oceanário** is Lisbon's most-visited attraction (p 18). Waterfront gardens, fountains, and walkways make it a pleasure to stroll here, and there's plenty of public artwork to admire, including works by British sculptor Antony Gormley and Icelandic pop artist Erró. The twin towers São Gabriel and São Rafael are among Portugal's tallest at 360 feet, their look inspired by ship sails. *Metro: Oriente. Bus: 705, 708, 725, 728, 744, 758, 782.* ●

A ride in a cable car (telecabine) provides bird's-eye views of the Tagus River and Parque das Nações.

The Best
Neighborhood Walks

The Alfama

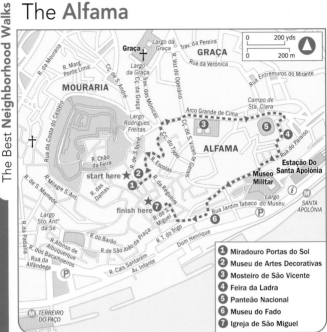

1. Miradouro Portas do Sol
2. Museu de Artes Decorativas
3. Mosteiro de São Vicente
4. Feira da Ladra
5. Panteão Nacional
6. Museu do Fado
7. Igreja de São Miguel

Hilly Alfama is the birthplace of the city, an ancient neighborhood with a meandering street plan that recalls the Arab medina it once was. This is the cradle of Lisbon's earthy *fado* music, a tightly knit district with a strong character and sense of community. We visited some of Alfama's highlights in chapters 1 and 2, but this tour is designed for a more intimate insight. You'll see fresh wash flapping from window lines, hear neighbors chatting across narrow lanes, and smell sardines grilling on doorstep barbecues. But Alfama is changing fast, as booming tourism turns family homes into vacation apartments. START: **Largo Portas do Sol.**

❶ ★★ Miradoura Portas do Sol. Alfama is laid out before you from this marvelous viewpoint. It's one of the most photogenic views of Lisbon, with the red rooftops of the old neighborhood, the towers and domes of the churches, strategically positioned palm trees, and the blue expanse of the Tagus beyond. Adding to the charm, little yellow

streetcars rattle by every few minutes. Less appealing are the pickpockets who operate here. Take care of your pockets and purses. *Tram: 12, 28.*

❷ ★★ Museu de Artes Decorativas. Across the street is the baroque Azurara Palace, which houses an array of furniture, textiles,

Previous page: Exploring the streets of Lisbon after a tram ride.

Sao Vicente statue at Miradouro das Portas do Sol.

tiles, porcelain, and glassware that offers an insight into 18th-century aristocratic life. Even more fascinating are the ateliers where the craftsmen and women preserve centuries of know-how in silver plating, leather book-binding, cabinet-making, and 15 other artist fields. The collection and the workshops are run by a foundation set up by banker Ricardo Espírito Santo Silva (1900–1955) with the aim of keeping traditional crafts alive. You can tour the workshops to watch the artisans in action and purchase their work, including reproductions of the museum exhibits. *Largo das Portas do Sol, 2. www.fress.com. ☎ 21 881 46 00. Admission 4€ adults; 2€ students. Wed–Mon 10am–5pm. Guided workshop tours (15€) Tues and Wed 11am and 3pm, Thurs 3pm; other times by appointment. Tram: 12, 28.*

③ ★★★ **Mosteiro de São Vicente de Fora.** Portugal's first king built a church here during his successful siege of Arab-held Lisbon; tombs of a couple of Teutonic knights who helped him are inside. Work on the current building in the grand Renaissance style began in 1583, during Portugal's 6-decade Spanish occupation. Ironically, it holds the tombs of the family who kicked the Spanish out and ruled up to 1910—14 Braganza monarchs are buried there. The church takes its name from St. Vincent, one of Lisbon's patrons and from the fact that it was outside (*fora*) the city walls. The church's white limestone facade dominates Alfama's skyline,

with great views from the roof. The interior is filled with baroque paintings and sculptures, and the magnificent sacristy is clad in marble. Perhaps the biggest attraction, though, are the tens of thousands of blue-and-white tiles (*azulejos*) painted with historical scenes and, rather strangely, illustrations of the children's fables published in the 1600s by French writer Jean de La Fontaine. The tiles are some of the best examples of this particularly Portuguese art form. *Largo de São Vicente. ☎ 21/888-5652. Admission 4€ adults; 2.50€ seniors and ages 12–21; free for children 11 and under. Tues–Sun 10am–5pm. Tram: 28.*

★ **World's Oldest Traffic Sign?** One of the curiosities of Alfama, this carved stone plaque in narrow Rua do Salvador is supposedly the world's oldest traffic sign. Dating back to 1668, it tells drivers that, by order of the king, "carriages and litters" that come through Salvador gate have to go back the same way. *Tram: 28.*

Monastery of St. Vincent.

❹ ★★ **Feira da Ladra.** Visit on a Tuesday or Saturday, and the broad open space behind São Vicente fills up with Lisbon's popular flea market. Its name translates as the "robber woman's fair." It's fun to browse the seemingly endless mix of bric-a-brac, handicrafts, junk, and genuine antiques on offer. Some of the better stuff can be found in the old covered-market building in the center of the square. Among the many cafes around the market, **As Marias com Chocolate** has a sunny terrace and lots of chocolate cakes. *Campo de Santa Clara. Tues and Sat 9am–6pm. Tram: 28.*

❺ ★ **Panteão Nacional.** The National Pantheon, just beside the market ground, is the final resting place of Portugal's great and good. Presidents and poets are buried there. Among the more recent arrivals are *fado* singer Amália Rodrigues (1920–1990), soccer great Eusébio (1942–2014), and Gen. Humberto Delgado, an opposition hero murdered by the dictatorship's secret police in 1966. That was also the year this great white-domed church—originally called after St. Engrácia—was finished, almost 300 years after work started. Even today the Portuguese refer to never-ending tasks as *obras* (works) *de Santa Engrácia.* Richly decorated in multicolored marble, the interior also has monuments to (but not the bones of) Discoveries-era heroes such as Vasco da Gama. More spectacular views from the roof. *Campo de Santa Clara.* ☎ *21/885-4820. Admission 3€ adults; 1.50€ seniors and ages 15–25; free for ages 14 and under. Tues–Sun 10am–5pm. Tram: 28.*

❻ ★★ **Museu do Fado.** Walk down **Rua dos Remédios**, one of Alfama's most emblematic streets, lined with little shops and *fado* bars, to reach the museum dedicated to the city's favorite musical genre (p 48). It's located in an old water-pumping station and recounts *fado's* evolution from mean-street serenade to UNESCO World Heritage icon. It holds interactive displays, old guitars, theater bills, and artworks, including at least one national treasure: José Malhoa's portrait of bohemian tavern life, *O Fado.* There's a shop well-stocked with CDs and a good café/restaurant. *Largo do Chafariz de Dentro, 1 www.museudofado.pt.* ☎ *21/ 882-3470. Admission 5€ adults; 3€ seniors and ages 6–30; free for children 5 and under. Tues–Sun 10am–5:30pm. Tram: 28. Bus: 728, 735, 759, 794.*

❼ ★ **Igreja de de São Miguel.** Unfortunately, this pretty little white church in the heart of Alfama is only open briefly each week. Behind its simple white facade is a jewel-box interior glowing with gold leaf. It is one of the city's best examples of *talho dourado,* a technique of coating ornate wood carvings in gold, dating back to a 17th-century gold rush in Portugal's Brazilian colonies. *Largo de São Miguel.* ☎ *21/886-6559. Free admission. Wed and Fri 4pm–6pm; Sun 8–10am. Tram: 28.* The Alfama text to continue on this page.

Fado guitar.

Sé

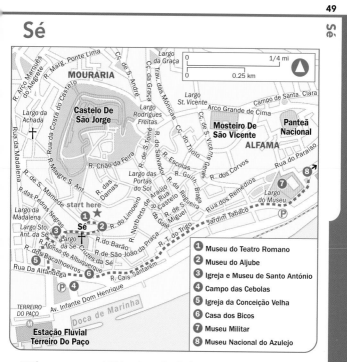

1 Museu do Teatro Romano
2 Museu do Aljube
3 Igreja e Museu de Santo António
4 Campo das Cebolas
5 Igreja da Conceição Velha
6 Casa dos Bicos
7 Museu Militar
8 Museu Nacional do Azulejo

The area around Lisbon's cathedral is among the city's oldest, rich in archeological remains from Roman and medieval times. We'll stroll streets soaked in history, then take a short trip along the riverbank to an out-of-center treasure. START: **Museu do Teatro Romano, Rua de São Mamede, 3 A; Tram 12, 28; Bus 737.**

1 ★ **Museu do Teatro Romano.** The 1755 earthquake led to the discovery of a Roman theater under the debris. With seating for 4,000, it reveals the importance of Olisipo as an outpost of the empire. Built during the reign of Augustus (63 B.C.–14), the theater was abandoned in the 4th century. The museum exhibits the archaeological finds and uses multimedia displays to tell the story of Roman Lisbon. *Rua de São Mamede, 3 A.* ☎ *21/581-8530. Admission 3€ adults; 1.50€ seniors; free students and children 12 and under; free general admission Sun until 2pm. Tues–Sun 10am–5:30pm. Tram: 12, 28. Bus: 737.*

2 ★ **Museu do Aljube.** An altogether different museum. This grim building was used as a prison since the Middle Ages—its name comes from the Arabic for "pit." From 1928 to 1965, the dictatorship detained and tortured political prisoners here. It's now a museum of "Resistance and Freedom" showing the history of the dictatorship, the suffering of prisoners, and the resistance movement that led to the democratic revolution of 1974. *Rua Augusto Rosa, 42. www.museudoaljube.pt.*

☎ 21/581-8535. Admission 3€ adults; free students and children 12 and under; free general admission Sun until 2pm. Daily 10am–6pm. Tram: 12, 28. Bus: 737.

3 ★ Igreja e Museu de Santo António. The rest of the Christian world may know him as St. Anthony of Padua, after the Italian city where he died, but for *Lisboetas* the saintly friar is one of theirs. His festival day on June 13 is the city's biggest party. In 1195, Anthony is believed to have been born where this pretty baroque church now stands next to Lisbon Cathedral (p 8). The museum tells the story of his life and holds venerated relics of the saint. *Largo de Santo António da Sé. www.stoantoniolisboa.com.* ☎ 21/886-9145. *Museum admission 3€ adults; 1.50€ seniors; free students and children 12 and under; free general admission Sun until 2pm. Church: Mon–Fri 8am–7pm; Sat–Sun 8am–8pm. Museum Tues–Sun 10am–5:30pm. Tram: 12, 28. Bus: 737.*

4 ★ Campo das Cebolas. The "Field of Onions" was once a medieval vegetable market, located between the cathedral and the river. For years it was a parking lot, but in 2017 was transformed into a cheerful garden with lawns, trees, and a playground. It's surrounded by historic buildings on three sides and features restaurants and cafes with outside seating. *Metro: Terreiro do Paço. Bus: 728, 735, 759, 781, 782.*

5 ★ Igreja da Conceição Velha. In the early 1500s King Manuel I ordered a church built here on the site of a former synagogue. It was the city's second-largest but was almost completely destroyed in the earthquake. What survives is the magnificent Manueline-style doorway, complete with

A Renaissance-style facade of stone spikes distinguishes the Casa dos Bicos.

floral designs, mythical beats, holy statues, and maritime mementos. The interior is rather modest, except for the dramatic ceiling in blue, gold, and white. *Rua da Alfândega, 108. Daily 10am–5pm. Metro: Terreiro do Paço. Tram: 15, 25. Bus: 728, 735, 759, 781, 782.*

6 ★ Casa dos Bicos. This noble residence built in 1523 for the family of the viceroy of Portuguese India was one of the few downtown buildings to survive the quake. Its unusual facade of stone spikes (*bicos*) was inspired by Renaissance Italy. It's home to the José Saramago Foundation, named for the late Nobel Prize–winning novelist, who died in 2010. His ashes are buried under an olive tree in front of the building. A museum holds archaeological remains, exhibition spaces, and a shop dedicated to the writer. *Rua dos Bacalhoeiros, 10.* ☎ 21/880-2040. *Admission 3€*

The Military Museum.

adults; 2€ students; free seniors and children 12 and under. Mon-Sat 10am–5:30pm. Metro: Terreiro do Paço. Bus: 728, 735, 759, 781, 782.

7 ★ kids Museu Militar. Lisbon's military museum is the city's oldest, dating back to the 1840s and still run by the army. It needs a facelift, and information in English is scant, but the building—a former arsenal—and the collection are impressive. It includes the sword wielded by King João I in 14th-century battles with Spanish invaders, Discoveries- era cannons, and a room dedicated to Portuguese troops in WWI. It's located by the river in front of the Santa Apolónia railroad station. *Largo do Museu da Artilharia.* ☎ 21/884-2453. Admission 3€; 1€ students and children 12 and under; free general admission Sun until 2pm. Tue-Sun 10am-4.15pm. Metro: Santa Apolónia; Bus: 712, 728, 734, 735, 759, 781, 794.

8 ★★★ Museu Nacional do Azulejo. Wherever you go in Lisbon you'll see *azulejos*. The painted ceramic tiles are used to decorate buildings inside and out, from ancient churches to modern Metro stations. The best place to understand this thoroughly Portuguese art form is this museum situated in a gem of a 16th-century convent in Lisbon's riverside Madre de Deus neighborhood. The collection contains tiles dating back over 600 years. Highlights include a giant panel showing Lisbon before the great earthquake of 1755 and the fabulous **Madre de Deus** convent church filled with blue-and-white tiles and carvings covered in gold leaf. It's well worth hopping on a bus to this out-of-the-way neighborhood between downtown and the Parque das Nações. *Rua da Madre de Deus, 4.* ☎ 21/810-0340. Admission 5€ adults; 2.50€ seniors and students; free for children 12 and under. Tues–Sun 10am–6m. Bus: 718, 742, 794.

The beautiful tiled interior of the Madre de Deus church inside the Museu Nacional do Azulejo.

The Grand Avenues

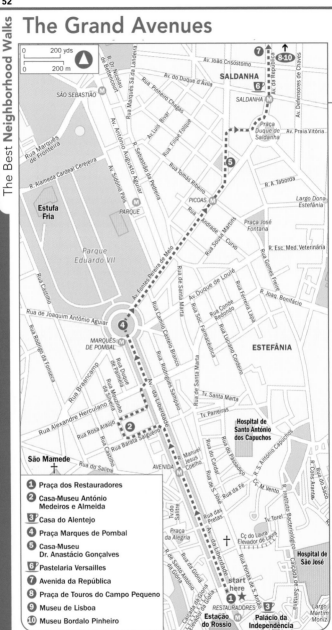

1 Praça dos Restauradores

2 Casa-Museu António Medeiros e Almeida

3 Casa do Alentejo

4 Praça Marques de Pombal

5 Casa-Museu Dr. Anastácio Gonçalves

6 Pastelaria Versailles

7 Avenida da República

8 Praça de Touros do Campo Pequeno

9 Museu de Lisboa

10 Museu Bordalo Pinheiro

This walk takes you along an axis of the grand 19th-century boulevards running from downtown toward the airport. There's plenty of shopping opportunities here, but also some quirky museums, delightful cafes, and a glimpse of another side of Lisbon. It's quite a long walk, but you can always jump on the bus and Metro lines that run along the route. START: **Praça dos Restauradores.**

The Monument to the Restorers obelisk in the Praça dos Restauradores.

❶ ★ Praça dos Restauradores. The obelisk in the center of this busy square, the Monument to the Restorers, honors fighters for the restoration of Portugal's independence in 1640, after 60 years of Spanish rule. The square marks the start of the Avenida da Liberdade, Lisbon's main shopping drag (p 79). Two imposing former movie houses—the 1930s Eden and the 1950s Condes—face off across the square. One is now a hotel, the other a Hard Rock Café. The most striking building, however, is the Palácio Foz, a patrician, pink-hued residence with mirrored salons inspired by Versailles. It contains a tourist office, a small museum of Portuguese sports, and a branch of the cinema museum showing classic children films. Most of the building is not normally open to the public, but there are regular guided visits and concerts in some of the grandest rooms. New in 2019: a music museum. Next door is a funicular heading up to the Bairro Alto. *Metro: Restauradores. Bus: 709, 711, 732, 736, 746, 783.*

❷ ★★ Casa-Museu António Medeiros e Almeida. Paintings by Delacroix and Tiepolo; one of Europe's biggest collections of timepieces, including a magnificent silver and lapis lazuli clock gifted to Sissi, Empress of Austria by Prince Ludwig of Bavaria; and Napoleon's tea set are just some of the treasures of this delightful museum. It's all housed in a mansion that was once home to the collector, business tycoon António de Medeiros e Almeida (1895–1986). Like visiting a private home stacked with fabulous decorative arts, it's one of the city's best-kept secrets. *Rua Rosa Araújo, 41. www.casa-museumedeirose almeida.pt.* ☎ *21/354-7 892. Admission 5€ adults; 3€ seniors; free for 18 and under 18s; free general admission Sat before 1pm. Mon–Sat 10am–4:30pm. Metro: Marquês de Pombal. Bus: 706, 709, 720, 727, 738, 774*

❸ ★★ Casa do Alentejo. Since the 1930s this splendid 17th-century place just off Avenida de Liberdade has been a club for people from the southern Alentejo region who now live in Lisbon. The building has an exotic neo-Moorish courtyard that's definitely worth a visit. Unfortunately, the main upstairs restaurant often falls short of the region's high culinary standards. Better to

The neo-Moorish courtyard of the Casa do Alentejo.

snack in the ground-floor tavern, which has a fine selection of cheeses, cured meats, and small dishes, like roast pork with paprika and garlic. *Rua Portas de Santo Antão, 58. www.casadoalentejo.com. pt.* ☎ *21/340-5140. $.*

④ ★ **Praça Marquês de Pombal.** This busy traffic hub rotates around a 130-foot monument to Sebastião José de Carvalho e Melo (1699–1782), the Marquis of Pombal, a towering figure in Portuguese history. As prime minister, he led reconstruction efforts after the great earthquake. The no-frills Pombaline architectural style of the Baixa was named after him. The traffic circle lies between Avenida da Liberdade and Eduardo VII Park (p 20). *Metro: Marquês de Pombal. Bus: 707, 712, 723, 727, 732, 736, 744, 748, 753, 783.*

⑤ ★ **Casa-Museu Dr. Anastácio Gonçalves.** Another art collector's residence turned into a museum, this award-winning Art Nouveau home is a survivor in an area of skyscraper hotels and office blocks. It was built for José Malhoa, a leading 19th-century artist, and later acquired by ophthalmologist António Anastácio Gonçalves, who amassed a collection of some 3,000 artworks with a focus on Chinese porcelain and Portuguese paintings. *Avenida 5 de Outubro, 6-8.* ☎ *21/354-0823. Admission 3€ adults; 1.50€ seniors and students; free for children 12 and under; free general admission Sun before 1pm. Tues–Sun 10am–1pm & 2–6pm. Metro: Saldanha. Bus: 701, 720, 727, 732, 738, 745.*

⑥ ★★★ **Pastelaria Versailles.** Lisbon's most beautiful cafe opened in 1922. The gleaming interior of mirrors, carved woodwork, and stained glass recalls the French palace of the same name. Waist-coated waiters whisk trays of tea and wonderful cakes to crowds of regular customers. The dining room on a raised section at the back is renowned for its sirloins. This classic European cafe recently opened branches in Belém and at Lisbon Airport. *Avenida da República 15-A.* ☎ *21/354-6340. $$.*

Monument to the Marques de Pombal.

View of Garden Central Avenue near Republic Square.

❼ ★★ Avenida da República.
Traffic hurtles along this mile-long thoroughfare into the city, but it has interesting shops and cafes and some architectural gems. It starts at **Praça do Duque de Saldanha** dominated by the bronze statue of a civil-war hero and surrounded by a couple of modern shopping malls. On the corner of leafy Avendia Duque de Avila, check out the **Pastelaria Sequeira,** founded in 1902, and the **Pérola do Chaimite,** a grocer specializing in fine coffees since 1940. **Galeto** at No. 14 is a delicious retro diner open from 7am to 3:30am, and **Casa Xangai** at No. 19 has been dressing the children of discerning *Lisboetas* since 1953. There are splendid Art Nouveau houses at No. 23 and No. 38. *Metro: Saldanha, Campo Pequeno. Bus: 727, 736, 738, 744, 783, 798.*

❽ ★ Praça de Touros do Campo Pequeno. Whatever your thoughts on bullfighting, it is hard to ignore Lisbon's bullring. Bright red and crowned with onion domes in an 1890s approximation of Arabian style, it's been nicknamed

Lisbon's Kremlin. Unlike in Spain, bulls are not killed in Portuguese bullfights, but they are stabbed with spears—thus the calls for a ban. The building holds a museum on bullfighting history and offering tours of the ring. As well as *corridas,* concerts by international and Portuguese stars are held here. In the basement is a shopping mall and cinema complex. Among several good restaurants, **Rubro** specializes in Spanish-style aged beef. *Centro de Lazer Campo Pequeno. www.campopequeno.com.* ☎ *21/799-8450. Museum admission 5€ adults; 4€ seniors; free for children 12 and under. Daily 10am–1pm and 2–7pm (until 6pm Nov–Mar). Metro: Campo Pequeno. Bus: 727, 736, 738, 744, 749, 754, 756, 783.*

❾ ★ Museu de Lisboa. At the far end of Avenida da República is the long **Campo Grande park** with the main university campus on its western side. Just beyond is the white neoclassical facade of **Palácio Pimenta,** home of the Lisbon city museum. The collection runs from Stone Age arrowheads to ceramic

Campo Pequeno bullring.

folk art. Pride of place goes to the painting collection, featuring views of cosmopolitan Lisbon before the 1755 earthquake. *Campo Grande 245 www.museudelisboa.pt. ☎ 21/751-3200. Admission 3€ adults; 1.5€ seniors; free students and children 12 and under; free general admission Sun before 2pm. Tues–Sun 10am–5:30pm. Metro: Campo Grande. Bus: 701, 717, 731, 735, 736, 738, 747, 750, 755, 767, 778, 783, 796, 798.*

⑩ ★★ **Museu Bordalo Pinheiro.** Across the park is a little museum dedicated to an idiosyncratic artist who's suddenly become internationally fashionable. Rafael Bordalo Pinheiro (1846–1905) was a dandy and caricaturist who poked fun at Portuguese society, but he's best known for founding a pottery factory. It still produces his designs of shiny bright ceramics, often with animal or vegetable themes. His cabbage-leaf fruit bowls, giant tomato tureens, and life-size black cat sculptures are must-have items in hipster homes. This is the place to discover more about their creator. A shop is on-site. *Campo Grande, 382 ☎ 21/581-8540. Admission 3€; 1.5€ seniors and students; free for children 12 and under; free general admission Sun before 2pm. Tues–Sun 10am–5:30pm. Metro: Campo Grande. Bus: 701, 717, 731, 735, 736, 738, 747, 750, 755, 767, 778, 783, 796, 798.*

Baixa

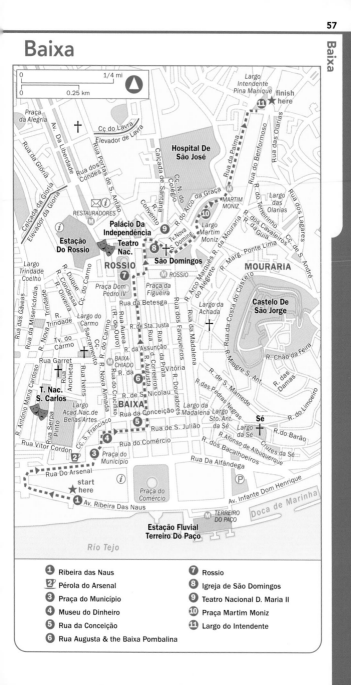

1. Ribeira das Naus
2. Pérola do Arsenal
3. Praça do Município
4. Museu do Dinheiro
5. Rua da Conceição
6. Rua Augusta & the Baixa Pombalina
7. Rossio
8. Igreja de São Domingos
9. Teatro Nacional D. Maria II
10. Praça Martim Moniz
11. Largo do Intendente

Unlike the winding lanes of Alfama, the Baixa's grid-like lay-out makes it easy to navigate. This tour takes you to one of the most diverse parts of the city, to the site of some of the darkest moments in Portugal's history as well as premium shopping streets. START: **Av. Ribeira das Naus. Metro: Cais do Sodré. Tram: 15, 25. Bus: 714, 728, 732, 735, 736, 760, 774,781, 782.**

The banks of the Tagus River along Ribeira dos Naus Avenue.

❶ ★★ **Ribeira das Naus.** This waterfront promenade was land-scaped in 2013 and is now a favorite spot for a relaxing stroll. It has sweeping river views, terrace cafes, and broad lawns. What look like trenches cut into the grass are the remains of naval dockyards, uncovered during the redevelopment work. This is where *naus*, sailing ships, that spear-headed the voyages of discoveries, were built. The navy's headquarters is still located here. Although the concrete ramp running down the Tagus has become a popular sun-bathing spot, rough currents and pollution mean no swimming. *Metro: Cais do Sodré. Tram: 15, 25. Bus: 714, 728, 732, 735, 736, 760, 774, 781, 782.*

❷ ★★ **Pérola do Arsenal.** The pungent whiff of dried fish greets you as you walk past this empo-rium, selling traditional Portuguese produce since 1952. As well as bac-alhau (salt cod), it sells dried octo-pus, barrels of tuna, and tins of sardines. Vintage wines are lined up behind the marble-topped counter. Senhor Rui and his team also have sacks of beans, stacks of yam, and jars of palm oil and hot piri-piri spice, making this place a favorite with Lisbon's African community.

Rua do Arsenal 94. www.perolado arsenal.com. ☎ *21/342-7938.*

❸ ★ **Praça do Município.** City Hall looks over this fine neoclassical plaza, which is covered in Lisbon's trademark black-and-white paving stones. In 1910, revolutionaries pro-claimed a new republican era from the balcony of the City Hall after deposing the last king, Manuel II. *Metro: Baixa-Chiado. Bus: 706, 728, 735, 781, 782.*

❹ ★★ **kids Museu do Dinheiro.** The Museum of Money sits in a for-mer church that for decades formed part of the Central Bank, holding Portugal's gold reserves in the vaults. The space is spectacular and the exhibits surprisingly fascinating, telling the history of currency from Ancient Greek coins to gold ingots from colonial Brazil and banknotes from around the world. The high-light for many may be picking up a 26-pound gold bar, estimated to be worth around 500,000€. You reach it through a small hole in a 7-ton safe door. Kids will love the interactive displays, where they can print their own bank notes and run checks for possible forgeries. Another attraction: 13th-century city walls uncovered in the basement during restoration work. *Largo de São Julião. www.museudodinheiro.pt.* ☎ *21/ 321-3240. Free admission. Wed–Sat 10am–6pm. Metro: Baixa-Chiado. Tram: 15, 25. Bus: 706, 711, 728, 735, 759, 774, 781, 782, 783, 794.*

5 ★★ Rua da Conceição. This street running through the Baixa is full of time machines. Step into any one of the scattering of tiny haberdashery stores (*retrosarias*) and you'll be transported to a bygone age. They are a delight, selling buttons, threads, ribbons, and balls of wool and seemingly unchanged from when they opened over 100 years ago. Among the most engaging are **Bijou** at No. 91; **Adriano Coelho** at No. 121-123; **Brilhante** at No. 79; **Alexandre Bento** at No. 67; and **Nardo** at No. 62. Once there were many more, and fans fret over how long the remaining old-school shops can survive.

6 ★★★ Rua Augusta & the Baixa Pombalina. Pedestrianized Rua Augusta is the main street running through the Baixa Pombalina—the grid of streets in the austere style of mostly five-story buildings imposed by the Marquis of Pombal after the earthquake.

Running from Rossio to the Triumphal Arch and into **Praça do Comércio** (p 8), it's always packed with locals and tourists perusing the shops and watching the array of street performers. There are lots of big international brands, but also some quintessentially Portuguese retailers like **Casa Pereira da Conceição** at No. 102, specializing in hand fans and coffee beans; **Madeira House,** selling lace and embroidery at No. 133; or the **Benfica Official Store** for soccer fans at No. 147.

Many of the streets parallel or perpendicular to Rua Augusta take their names from the tradespeople

Bustling Rua Augusta and the Triumphal Arch.

who used to work there: *ouro* (gold), *douradores* (goldsmiths), *prata* (silver), *sapateiros* (cobblers), *correeiros* (saddlers), and *fanqueiros* (drapers). Few survive, but you'll find plenty of interesting stores to explore and lots of restaurants. Beware those tourist traps where waiters try to drag you in waving photo menus—they often add hidden costs to your bill. Among the good bets for eating in the area are **Marisqueira Uma** (for seafood) and **A Merendinha do Arco,** (serving traditional lunchtime snacks), both on Rua dos Sapateiros, or—for a change— **Tasca Kome,** a popular Japanese joint on Rua da Madalena. *Metro: Baixa-Chiado, Rossio. Tram: 15, 25, 28. Bus: 728, 735, 759, 774, 781, 782.*

7 ★★ Rossio. This is Lisbon's Times Square or Piccadilly Circus, a bustling meeting place complete with fountains, pavement cafes, and traditional shops. The wavy black-and-white paving has inspired walkways across the Portuguese-speaking world from Macao to Copacabana.

Rossio's official name, Praça Dom Pedro IV, honors the king of Portugal and first emperor of Brazil, whose statue stands atop a 90-foot column. There is apparently no truth in the urban legend that the statue is actually of Emperor Maximilian of Mexico, recycled after his execution in 1867.

A fountain in Rossio Square.

Historic cafes **Nicola** and the **Suiça,** facing each other across the square, were popular during WWII with refugees who poured into neutral Portugal. Peggy Guggenheim and Max Ernst were patrons of the Suiça, but at press time its future was in doubt amid plans to turn the building into a hotel.

Take a peek through the archway at the southern end of the square and you'll find what is possibly the world's prettiest pornographic cinema. **Animatógrafo do Rossio** was one of Lisbon's first movie houses, opening in 1908. Its Art Nouveau facade is a gem. Since 1994, however, it only shows a particular type of movie.

Beyond the northwest corner of the square, Rossio Station is the terminus of the rail line to Sintra. It was built in 1887 in the neo-Manueline style, which sought to recapture the glories of the Discoveries era with horseshoe-shaped doors lined with elaborate motifs. *Metro: Rossio. Bus: 711, 732, 736, 746, 759, 783.*

⑧ ★★ Igreja de São Domingos. This church was never fully repaired after a devastating fire in 1957. Where once were baroque paintings and gilded carvings are bare walls and soot-darkened columns. It is an eerie place to visit, even more so because of its dark history. In Easter 1506, an argument broke out in the church between a Jew who had newly converted to Christianity and other worshipers in what was then one of the biggest

The horseshoe-shaped entrance doors to the Rossio railway station.

Martim Moniz Square.

churches in Lisbon. The dispute sparked a wave of mob violence that targeted the Jewish community. King Manuel, who was out of the city, eventually sent in the royal guard to quell the violence, but not before an estimated 2,000 Jews were murdered. More horrors were to come. Thirty years later, Manuel's successor João III invited the Holy Inquisition to Portugal. Over the next 250 years it would persecute people suspected of deviating from Catholic teaching, ordering around 1,200 people to be burned at the stake. The executions would often take place right here in Rossio. Many victims were so-called "New Christians"—Jews who had converted to avoid being expelled from the country. In 1987, President Mário Soares asked the Jewish community for forgiveness on behalf of Portugal. A memorial was placed in front of the church in 2006, and 2 years later Lisbon held a ceremony there, declaring itself "City of Tolerance," open to all races and religions. *Largo de São Domingos.* ☎ *21/342-8275. Admission free. Daily 7:30am–7pm. Metro: Rossio. Bus: 711, 732, 736, 746, 759, 783.*

⑨ ★ Teatro Nacional D. Maria II. Occupying the north end of Rossio is the stately facade of Portugal's National Theater. It was built in the 1840s on the site of the Inquisition's headquarters. Guided tours of its grand interior are given every Monday. Inside the arcaded lobby are a bookshop and a good restaurant (p 130). *Praça D. Pedro IV. www.tndm.pt.* ☎ *21/325-0835. Guided tours Mon 11am (8€ adults; 5€ seniors and students). Metro: Rossio. Bus: 711, 732, 736, 746, 759, 783.*

⑩ ★ Praça Martim Moniz. This sprawling square is not Lisbon's prettiest. It's surrounded by ugly modern buildings, but it's the center point of the city's most diverse neighborhood, home to communities originating in China, South Asia, and Africa. You'll find Chinese and Indian grocers and lots of simple but tasty Chinese restaurants (Mi Dai, with mains around 5€, at Calçada da Mouraria, 7, is a favorite). In the center of the square are stands selling street food from around the world and there are regular markets and concerts at weekends. *Metro: Martim Moniz. Tram: 12, 28. Bus: 708, 734, 736, 768.*

⑪ ★ Largo do Intendente. Until a few years ago, this was the capital's seediest redlight district and a place to avoid after dark. Now it's one of the city's most fashionable spots, with innovative stores like A Vida Portuguesa and Viúva Lamego (p 79), a beautifully restored Art Nouveau hotel (1908 Lisboa Hotel) (p 143), cafes, restaurants, craft markets, and street performers. *Metro: Martim Moniz. Tram: 12, 28. Bus: 708, 734, 736, 768.*

Fashionable Largo do Intendente.

Chiado

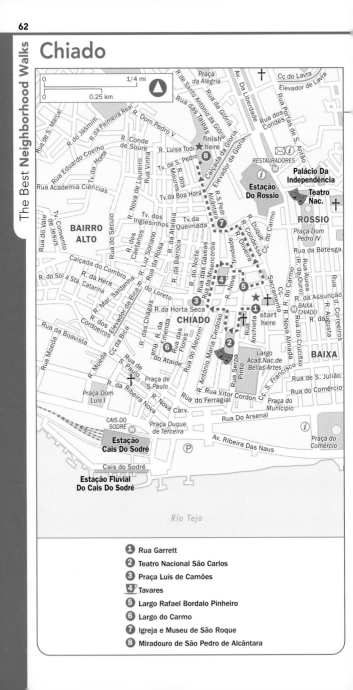

1. Rua Garrett
2. Teatro Nacional São Carlos
3. Praça Luís de Camões
4. Tavares
5. Largo Rafael Bordalo Pinheiro
6. Largo do Carmo
7. Igreja e Museu de São Roque
8. Miradouro de São Pedro de Alcântara

The venerable stores and cafes uptown in the Chiado district recall a bygone era captured in the novels of José Maria de Eça de Queirós and the poems of Fernando Pessoa. It's Lisbon's theater land and holds some some of the city's best restaurants and most elegant squares. START: **Rua Garrett. Metro: Baixa-Chiado. Tram: 28, 24.**

Rua Garrett in the heart of the trendy Chiado district.

❶ ★★★ **Rua Garrett.** The Chiado's steep main street is lined left and right with wonderful stores old and new. Check out the delectable pastries of **Alcôa** at No. 37; the ornate interior of **Tous** jewelers at No. 50; and the **Pequeno Jardim,** selling flowers at No. 61 since 1922. Many of the neighborhood bookstores are gone, but **Livraria Sá da Costa** remains, a labyrinth piled with antique volumes. At weekends an open-air book market is held next to the **Livraria Bertrand** (p 78).

Don't miss **Paris em Lisboa**, which opened in 1888 to import fancy French fabrics and now has three floors of high-quality household goods. Also take a look at the magnificent painted ceiling at the **Basílica dos Mártires,** halfway up on the left. *Baixa-Chiado. Tram: 28, 24.*

❷ ★★ **Teatro Nacional São Carlos.** Lisbon's opera house looks onto an airy square where outdoor concerts are held in summer. The cafe spilling out of the theater is run by chef José Avillez.

Theater of Sao Carlos.

Cafes in pretty Praça Luis de Camões.

The facade of São Carlos is a simple neoclassical combination of white brick archways and yellow walls. The auditorium inside is a rococo gem inspired by its famous Neapolitan namesake. First-class operatic and concert performances (p 128) are often on the calendar. Phone ahead to book guided tours. *Rua Serpa Pinto, 9. www.tnsc.pt.* ☎ *21/325-3045. Metro: Baixa-Chiado. Tram: 28.*

❸ ★★ **Praça Luís de Camões.** Walk past the storied Café A Brasileira (p 10) and take a look in the pair of baroque churches facing each other across the square. Beyond is the square named for the swashbuckling poet Luís de Camões (1524–1580) whose statue looms over it. His poem Os Lusíadas, a fantasy based on Vasco da Gama's voyage, is the national epic. Camões himself was a seafarer who lost an eye fighting in Morocco and supposedly saved the text of his great poem by holding it aloft as he swam from a shipwreck off the coast of Cambodia. The square is a lively meeting point, especially at night. Camões' rival as Portugal's greatest poet, Fernando Pessoa (1888–1935), has his own statue just down the hill seated outside A Brasileira. *Metro Baixa-Chiado. Tram: 28, 24. Bus: 758.*

❹ 🍴 ★★ **Tavares.** The oldest restaurant in Lisbon and one of the oldest in Europe opened in 1784. Its dining room is a glittering rococo confection of mirrors, chandeliers, and gilded stucco. The menu mixes Portuguese and international influences, with mains from 31€ to 38€. *Rua da Misericórdia, 37. www.restaurante tavares.pt.* ☎ *21/342-1112. $$$.*

❺ ★★ **Largo Rafael Bordalo Pinheiro.** This triangular plaza is filled with fashionable restaurants. Among them are a couple of hip Asian eateries (**Bao Bao** and **Nood**); **La Parisienne**, one of the city's best French bistros; and **Aqui Há Peixe,** serving classic Portuguese fish dishes. Boutiques include **Soul Mood** and **Gardenia**. Topping it all off, the north end of the square has one of Lisbon most beautiful tiled facades. Dating from the 1860s, it's covered with orange-and-cream *azulejos* depicting figures representing human endeavor and the natural elements. *Metro: Baixa-Chiado. Tram: 24. Bus: 758.*

❻ ★★ **Largo do Carmo.** One of Lisbon's most picturesque

Stone fountain in the Largo do Carmo square.

The gilded interior of the São Roque church.

squares lies beside the **Carmo convent** ruins (p 9). In the center is an 18th-century fountain, and the jacaranda trees bloom purple in the spring. It hasn't always been so tranquil. During the April 25, 1974, uprising, the National Republican Guard (GNR) headquarters here was besieged by revolutionary troops after the government sought refuge. The building was sprayed with a burst of machine gun fire before ministers surrendered, ending 46 years of dictatorship. Next to the **Santa Justa Elevator** (p 9) are great views. *Metro: Baixa-Chiado. Tram: 24. Bus: 758.*

7 ★★★ **Igreja e Museu de São Roque.** From the plain exterior you wouldn't guess the treasures within. This masterpiece combines two Portuguese art forms: *azulejo* tiles and *talha dourada* (gold-covered wood carving), which took off after a gold rush in the Brazilian colonies made king João V one of Europe's richest monarchs. The whole interior gleams with gold, but its crowning glory is the **Chapel of St. John,** which the king ordered from Rome and shipped here at enormous cost. It is a rococo fantasy in lapis lazuli, agate, alabaster, Carrara marble, gold, ivory, and more. The church was a headquarters for the Jesuits; an adjacent museum tells its story. *Largo Trindade Coelho. www.museu-saoroque.com.* ☎ *21/324-0869. Museum admission 2.50€ adults; free seniors, students, and ages 14 and under; free general admission Sun before 2pm. Oct–Mar Mon 2–5:30, Tues–Sun 10am–5:30pm; Apr–Sept Mon 2–6:30pm, Tues–Wed and Fri–Sun 10am--6:30pm, Thurs 10am–7:30pm. Tram: 24. Bus: 758.*

8 ★ **Miradouro de São Pedro de Alcântara.** A perfect place to finish your walk, this view point has a mini park and wonderful views across to Castelo de São Jorge. Across the road is a convent interior beautifully decorated with *azulejos. Rua São Pedro de Alcântara. Tram: 24. Bus: 758.*

Tram in Miradouro de São Pedro de Alcântara. Cais do Sodre text to continue on this page.

Belém, Ajuda, Alcântara

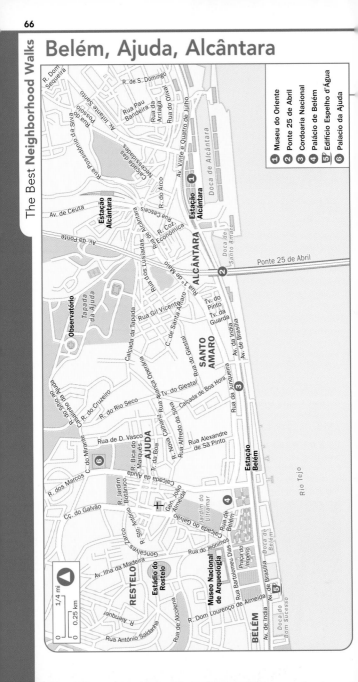

1 Museu do Oriente
2 Ponte 25 de Abril
3 Cordoaria Nacional
4 Palácio de Belém
5 Edifício Espelho d'Água
6 Palacio da Ajuda

We now take a closer look at the attractions in riverside Belém and the neighboring districts of Ajuda, with its truncated royal place, and Alcântara, with an exotic museum and waterfront restaurants. START: Museu do Oriente, Tram stop: 15.

❶ ★★★ kids **Museu do Oriente.** Down by the docks is a bulky, windowless building built in the 1940s to store salt cod. In 2008, it was transformed into a museum to celebrate Lisbon's 5 centuries of cultural and commercial exchanges with Asia. The dark spaces inside feature eclectic collections of treasures ranging from larger-than-life statues of Jesuit martyrs to suits of Samurai armor, Chinese snuff bottles, and rough-hewn ritual masks from East Timor. Regular temporary exhibitions showcase contemporary Asian artists. There are also concerts, and visitors can join workshops on themes ranging from Javanese percussion to origami and Indian cuisine. The top-floor restaurant serves a renowned weekend brunch. *Avenida Brasília, Doca de Alcântara.* 📞 *21/358-5200. Admission 6€ adults; 3.50€ seniors; 2.50€ students; 2€ youngsters 6–12; free for children 5 and under; free general admission Fri 6–9:30pm. Open Tues–Thurs and Sat–Sun 10am–5:30pm; Fri 10am–9:30pm. Train: Alcântara. Tram: 15, 18. Bus: 714, 738, 742.*

❷ ★★ kids **Ponte 25 de Abril.** Given its resemblance to the Golden Gate Bridge, it should come as no surprise to discover that the red suspension bridge spanning the Tagus was built by engineers from San Francisco in 1966. An observation desk 260 feet up on one of the pillars was opened in 2017, for a vertigo-inducing experience. A museum has high-tech exhibits and virtual-reality displays to explain the construction and workings of the bridge, which carries 150,000 cars and 157 trains over the Tagus on an average day. Just below the bridge, the **Doca de Santo Amaro,** is a pleasant area for strolling, with a row of riverside restaurants. *Avenida da Índia.* 📞 *21/111-7880. Admission 6€ adults; 4€ seniors and students; free for children 6 and under. May–Sept 10am–7:30pm; Oct–Apr 10am–5:30pm. Train: Alcântara. Tram: 15. Bus: 714, 727, 732, 751, 756.*

❸ ★ **Cordoaria Nacional.** Just inland from the new MAAT art museum (p 42) is a strange-looking building, just one story high and 150 feet wide, but more than 1,300 feet long. Lisboetas like to quiz visitors about what it was built for. The answer? Making ropes for sailing ships, which apparently needed to be stretched out to great lengths

The 25th April Bridge.

Portuguese Republican Guard performing changing of the guard ceremony at the Presidential Palace.

during the production process. Constructed in 1779, this yellow-hued building is used for antique shows and temporary exhibitions. *Avenida da Índia. Train: Belém. Tram: 15. Bus: 714, 727, 732, 751, 756.*

④ ★ **Palácio de Belém.** This pretty pink palace with great river views is the official residence of Portugal's president. Visitors can take guided tours Saturdays between 10:30am and 4pm. Otherwise, you can learn about Portugal's politics and modern history in the palace museum. At 11am on the third Sunday of each month, an impressive changing of the guard ceremony in front of the palace involves 160 members of the National Republican Guard in dress uniform, including cavalry units on white chargers. Between the palace and the river are formal gardens dominated by a towering monument to Afonso de Albuquerque (1453–1515) an empire-builder in Asia. *Praça Afonso de Albuquerque. www.museu. presidencia.pt.* ☎ *21/361-4980. Museum admission 2.50€ adults; 1.5€ seniors and students; free for ages 14 and under; free general admission Sun until 1pm. Tues–Sun 10am–5:30pm; Train: Belém. Tram: 15. Bus: 714, 727, 729, 751.*

⑤ ★★ **Edifício Espelho d'Água.** Located in an iconic modernist building from the 1940s and surrounded by water, this cool cultural space features exhibitions, concerts, and a store with a Brazilian flavor. The restaurant serves a contemporary cuisine with influences from as far afield as Japan, Morocco, and above all Brazil. *Avenida Brasilia, Edificio Espelho de Agua. http:// espacoespelhodeagua.com.* ☎ *21/301-0510. $$.*

⑥ ★★ **Palacio da Ajuda.** Moving up the hill and back in time we come to the last residence of Portugal's royal family before the presidents took over. After the 1755 earthquake, King José I was so shaken he refused to live under masonry and took to a wooden cabin, known as the "royal hut," up on this hillside. His daughter Queen Maria I eventually decided something grander was needed and work was begun on a colossal neoclassical stone palace. Work on the building was interrupted by the Napoleonic invasion, when the

Statue at the Ajuda Palace.

Dining room in the Ajuda Palace.

royals fled to Brazil, and then the Civil War (1828–1834). Then the money ran out. So what you see today looks like a grand rival to London's Buckingham Palace from the front, but from the back it's an abandoned construction site. Still, it makes an impressive visit, its sumptuous salons fully furnished with regal trappings, as if the royals were expected to return at any moment. Particularly impressive is the banquet room where the president still holds state dinners. In 2016, a 21€-million plan was launched to finish the construction by building a west wing to hold the royal jewels, currently stashed in vaults. It's due for completion in 2020, so there may be closures of some rooms during construction. *Largo da Ajuda. www.palacioajuda.gov.pt. ☎ 21/363-7095. Admission 5€ adults; 2.5€ seniors and students; free for ages 13 and under. Thurs–Tues 10am–5:30pm. Train: Belém. Bus: 729, 732, 742.*

São Bento, Príncipe Real & Amoreiras

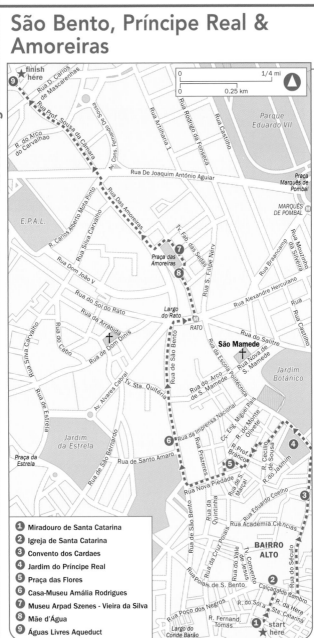

1. Miradouro de Santa Catarina
2. Igreja de Santa Catarina
3. Convento dos Cardaes
4. Jardim do Príncipe Real
5. Praça das Flores
6. Casa-Museu Amália Rodrigues
7. Museu Arpad Szenes - Vieira da Silva
8. Mãe d'Água
9. Águas Livres Aqueduct

These three neighboring districts are renowned for their shopping, charm, and tranquil gardens, as well as some great cafes, striking historical monuments, and intriguing museums.
START: **Miradouro de Santa Catarina. Tram: 28.**

Century-old white cedar in the garden of Príncipe Real.

❶ ★★ Miradouro de Santa Catarina.
In a city of great views this is one of the best, high up over the river and the rooftops. Sunsets here are spectacular. With lawns and a couple of cafes, it's a popular spot for young people, who gather in the evenings to drink beer and listen to street musicians. The miradouro is watched over by the brooding statue of Adamastor, a mythical giant who haunts the Cape of Good Hope in the epic poem Os Lusíadas. It's also next to the picturesque Bica neighborhood, with its famed funicular. *Largo do Rato. Metro: Rato. Bus: 6, 9, 58, 74.*

❷ ★★ Igreja de Santa Catarina.
Most tourists rattling past in Tram 28 ignore this 17th-century church by the tracks. That's a pity, because the interior is one of the most lavish in the city, decked out with carvings covered in Brazilian gold, a glorious rococo stucco-work ceiling, and paintings by Portugal's best painters of the baroque era. *Calçada do Combro 82.* ☎ *21/346-4443. Admission free. Daily 9am–noon, 2pm–5pm. Tram: 28.*

❸ ★★ Convento dos Cardaes.
The long, narrow Rua de O Século runs along the edge of the Bairro Alto towards Príncipe Real. Among its bookshops and art galleries is a hidden treasure: a convent that survived the earthquake and contains another church filled with baroque goldwork set off against blue-and-white-tiled panels and large-scale religious paintings. It's still a working convent, where nuns care for disabled women residents. A shop sells their homemade cakes, jams, and other products. *Rua de O Século 123.* ☎ *21/342-7525. Admission 5€ adults; 4€ seniors and students. Mon–Sat 2:30–5:30pm. Closed Aug. Tram: 24. Bus: 758, 773.*

❹ ★★ Jardim do Príncipe Real.
An oasis in the city's trendiest dining and shopping areas (p 79), this garden is filled with ornamental ponds and exotic trees, the most impressive of which is a 150-year-old cypress so wide that it's supported by an iron frame. You can sit at one of the many outdoor cafes, or go underground to visit a huge cistern, part of the 18th-century water system (p 72). The garden hosts

regular craft markets and a farmer's market on Saturdays. *Praça do Príncipe Real. Tram: 24. Bus 758, 773.*

⑤ ★★ Praça das Flores. This shady garden is a favorite place for locals to unwind. It's surrounded by restaurants and cafes, where you can sample organic pizza at **In Bocca al Lupo**, traditional dishes from central Portugal at **Bem Haja,** and Persian delights at **Cafeh Tehran.** *Palácio de São Bento.* ☎ *21/391-9000.*

⑥ ★★ Casa-Museu Amália Rodrigues. On a street containing Portugal's Parliament and Lisbon's best selection of antique shops is the home of *fado's* greatest singer (p 20). This three-story yellow house has been left largely as it was when Amália lived here up to her death in 1999. The diva's rags-to-riches story is told through thousands of her personal items including ritzy dresses, jewelry, and portraits. Amália's parrot still lives in the kitchen and occasionally says *"olá"* to visitors. *Rua de São Bento 193. www.amaliarodrigues.pt.* ☎ *21/397 1896. Admission 5€ adults; 3.50€ seniors and students; free for children 5 and under. Daily 10am–6pm. Metro: Rato. Bus: 707, 727.*

⑦ ★ Museu Arpad Szenes-Vieira da Silva. Maria Helena Vieira da Silva was perhaps Portugal's greatest 20th-century painter. The city of her birth has dedicated this museum to the painter and her Hungarian artist husband. It's housed in a former silk factory and displays Vieira da Silva's abstract works. *Praça das Amoreiras, 56. www.fasvs.pt.* ☎ *21/384-1490. Admission 5€ adults; 2.50€ students and retired; free for children 12 and under. Tues–Sun 10am–6pm. Metro: Rato. Bus: 706, 709, 713, 758, 720, 727, 738, 774.*

⑧ ★★★ kids Mãe d'Água & Águas Livres Aqueduct. Across the square is the Mãe d'Água (Mother of Water), a vast cistern built in the 1700s as a key part of the city water supply. It's now part of the award-winning Museum of Water. Inside it's like a flooded cathedral with columns supporting the high, arched roof emerging from the waters. The reservoir is the terminus of the great **⑨ Águas Livres aqueduct,** an engineering marvel whose giant arches stride over 11 miles into the city. It survived the earthquake and carried water to Lisbon until the 1960s. A talk along the 1,000-yard final and highest section is a unique experience. *Mãe d'Água: Praça das Amoreiras 10. www.epal. pt.* ☎ *21/810-0215. Admission 3€ adults; 2.50€ seniors and students; free for children 12 and under. Tues– Sun 10am–12:30pm and 1:30–5pm. Metro: Rato. Bus: 706, 709, 713, 758, 720, 727, 738, 774. Aquaduct: Calçada da Quintinha 6. Admission 3€ adults; 1.5€ seniors and students; for children 12 and under. Tues–Sun 10am–5:30pm. Bus: 742, 751, 758.* ●

The 18th-century Mother of Water reservoir, now part of the Museum of Water.

Shopping Best Bets

Best **Wine Shop**
★★ Garrafeira Nacional,
Rua de Santa Justa, 18 (p 83)

Best **Historic Store**
★★★ Casa das Velas do Loreto,
Avenida da Liberdade, 185 (p 83)

Best **Azulejos (tiles)**
★★★ Viúva Lamego, *Largo do
Intendente, 25 (p 79)*

Best **Souvenirs**
★★★ A Vida Portuguesa,
Largo do Intendente (p 82)

Best **Antiques**
★★★ Solar, *Rua D. Pedro V, 70
(p 78)*

Best **Posh Shopping**
★★ Avenida de Liberdade *(p 79)*

Best **Designer Shopping**
★★★ Príncipe Real *(p 79)*

Best **Mall**
★★★ Embaixada, *Praça do
Príncipe Real, 26 (p 80)*

Best **Jewelry**
★★ Leitão & Irmão, *Largo do
Chiado, 16 (p 83)*

Best **Portuguese Shoes**
★★★ Fly London, *Av. da
Liberdade, 230 (p 84)*

*Shopping in the public market of the
Mercado de Campo de Ourique.*

Best **Perfume**
★★★ Claus Porto, *Rua da
Misericórdia, 135 (p 83)*

Best **Hat Shop**
★★ Azevedo Rua, *Dom Pedro IV,
72–73 (p 81)*

Previous page: Rua Anchieta weekend book market in the Chiado district.

North of Center Shopping

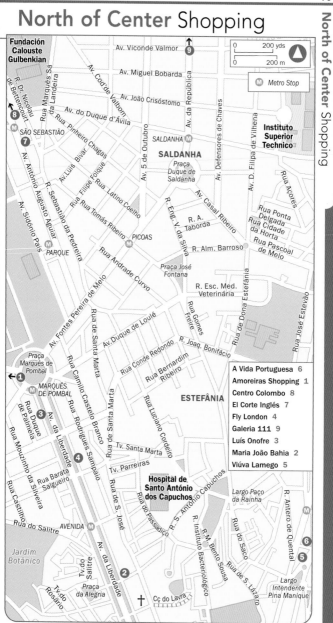

Fundación Calouste Gulbenkian

Av. Visconde Valmor

Av. Miguel Bobarda

Av. João Crisóstomo

Av. Cod de Valbom

Av. do Duque d'Ávila

Rua Marquês Sá da Bandeira

R. Dr. Nicolau de Bettencourt

SÃO SEBASTIÃO

Av. António Augusto Aguiar

Av. Sidónio Pais

Rua Pinheiro Chagas

Av. Luis Bivar

R. Sebastião da Pedreira

Rua Filipe Folque

Rua Latino Coelho

Rua Tomás Ribeiro

PICOAS

Rua Andrade Curvo

Av. 5 de Outubro

SALDANHA

Av. da República

Av. Defensores de Chaves

Av. D. Filipa de Vilhena

Instituto Superior Technico

SALDANHA

Praça Duque de Saldanha

Av. Casal Ribeiro

R. Eng. V. da Silva

R. A. Taborda

R. Alm. Barroso

Praça José Fontana

Rua Açores

Rua Ponta Delgada

Rua Cidade da Horta

Rua Pascoal de Melo

R. Esc. Med. Veterinária

Rua Gomes Freire

Rua de Dona Estefânia

Rua José Estevão

Av. Fontes Pereira de Melo

Rua de Santa Marta

Av. Duque de Loulé

Rua Conde Redondo

Rua Bernardim Ribeiro

R. Joaq. Bonifácio

Praça Marquês de Pombal

MARQUÊS DE POMBAL

Rua Duque de Palmela

Av. da Liberdade

Rua Camilo Castelo Branco

Rua Rodrigues Sampaio

Rua de Santa Marta

Rua Luciano Cordeiro

ESTEFÂNIA

Rua Mouzinho da Silveira

Rua Barata Salgueiro

Tv. Santa Marta

Tv. Parreiras

Rua Castilho

Rua do Salitre

AVENIDA

Jardim Botânico

Tv. do Salitre

Tv. do Rosário

Praça da Alegria

Av. da Liberdade

Rua de S. José

Hospital de Santo António dos Capuchos

Rua do Passadiço

R. S. António Capuchos

R. Instituto Bacteriológico

Largo Paço da Rainha

R. M. Bento Sousa

Rua do Saco

Rua de S. Lázaro

R. Antero de Quental

Largo Intendente Pina Manique

Cç do Lavra

A Vida Portuguesa	6
Amoreiras Shopping	1
Centro Colombo	8
El Corte Inglés	7
Fly London	4
Galeria 111	9
Luís Onofre	3
Maria João Bahia	2
Viúva Lamego	5

0	200 yds
0	200 m

Ⓜ Metro Stop

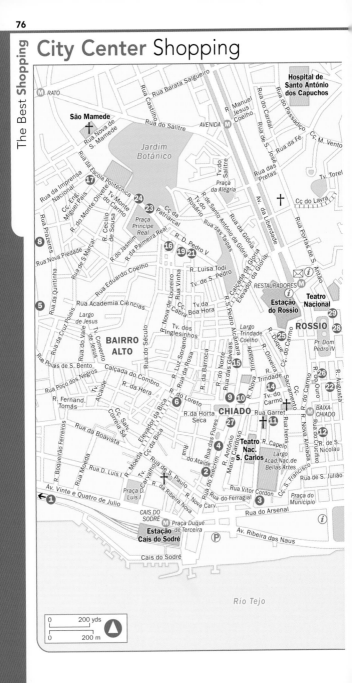

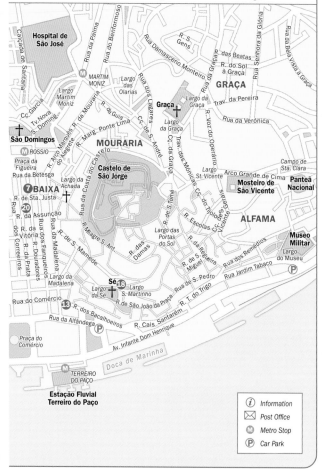

ⓘ	Information
✉	Post Office
Ⓜ	Metro Stop
Ⓟ	Car Park

Lisbon Shopping A to Z

Antiques & Art

★ Cavalo de Pau SÃO BENTO
This charming store in the heart of the antiques district sells a mix of vintage goods and its own retro designs, plus art objects from around the world and ceramics. *Rua de São Bento, 164. ww.cavalodepau. pt.* ☎ *21/396-6605. Metro: Rato. Tram: 28. Map p 76.*

★★ Galeria 111 CAMPO GRANDE   A leading light on the art scene since the 1960s. Cutting-edge exhibitions and a wide selection of works by contemporary artists from Portugal and beyond, including world-renowned Paula Rego. *Campo Grande, 113. www. 111.pt.* ☎ *21/797-7418. Metro: Cidade Universitária. Map p 75.*

★ Miguel Arruda SÃO BENTO
Top-class antiques beautifully presented in a palatial townhouse. The range is huge, from 18th-century furniture crafted from Brazilian

hardwood to delicate Chinese porcelain and saintly church statues. *Rua de São Bento, 356. www.arruda. pt.* ☎ *21/393-0714. Metro: Rato. Tram: 28. Map p 76.*

★★★ Solar PRÍNCIPE REAL
Around since the 1940s, Lisbon's oldest antiques shop is the place to buy antique *azulejos* (ceramic tiles). Its collection is a treasure trove with pieces dating back to the 15th century. *Rua D. Pedro V, 70. www.solar.com.pt.* ☎ *21/ 346-5522. Tram: 24. Map p 76.*

Books

★★★ Bertrand CHIADO   Officially the world's oldest bookstore, Bertrand opened in 1732 and is still going strong. The delightful maze of small rooms contains a little cafe and a selection of English books and magazines. It's sacred ground for literary *Lisboetas*, with branches around the city. *Rua Garrett, 73-75. www.bertrand.pt* ☎ *21/347-6122. Metro: Baixa-Chiado. See map p 76.*

★★★ Ler Devagar ALCÂNTARA
A landmark in the post-industrial LX Factory cultural zone. It's huge, located in an old print shop with books stacked around the vintage presses. The flying bicycle installation is an Instagram favorite. It has a limited selection of books in English. Cool cafe and regular cultural events. *Rua Rodrigues Faria 103. www.lerdevagar.com.* ☎ *21/325-9 992. Train: Alcantara-Mar. Tram 15, 18. Map p 76.*

★★ Palavra de Viajante BAIRRO ALTO   This little place is a traveler's delight. Novels, guides, memoirs, you name it—all are arranged by country. The selection is multilingual with many choices in English. The staff is very knowledgeable and

The world's oldest bookstore, Bertrand.

Ler Devagar Bookstore.

very helpful—looking for a thriller set in Lisbon? They'll know what to pick. *Rua de São Bento, 34. www. palavra-de-viajante.pt.* ☎ *21/395-0328. Tram; 28. Map p 76.*

Ceramics, Pottery & Tiles
★★ Fabrica Sant'Anna CHIADO A great place to buy *azulejos* since 1741. All are handmade, from exquisite individual tiles to elaborate panels covered in still-life or pastoral scenes to ceramic pots, vases, and basins. Aside from the flagship Chiado store, you can visit

the factory near Belém or even book a lesson to craft your own. *Rua do Alecrim, 95. www.santanna. com.pt.* ☎ *21/342-2537. Metro: Baixa-Chiado. Map p 76.*

★★★ Viúva Lamego INTEN-DENTE A really special place. This store, open since 1849, is covered in gloriously hued *azulejos*. Its tiles also cover buildings around the country, including many of Lisbon's Metro stations, and are treasured by artists and architects. Its selection includes both traditional and

Best Shopping Areas

Príncipe Real is Lisbon's most fashionable shopping district. It's lined with cool boutiques, antique shops, and design emporiums. **Avenida da Liberdade** is the city's grandest boulevard, filled with high-end fashion. The **Baixa** is a traditional shopping zone, with a mix of international brands, quirky traditional stores, and tourist traps. Up the hill to **Chiado**, Rua do Carmo and Rua Garrett are filled with international chains, but plenty of characterful local stores cling on, including its renowned antique bookstores. Away from downtown, the leafy **Alvalade** and **Campo de Ourique** neighborhoods offer an attractive mix of stores and excellent food markets. A plethora of large, modern malls rings the city center.

contemporary designs of the highest quality. There's a second store at the factory in Sintra. *Largo do Intendente, 25. www.viuvalamego. com.* ☎ *21/2 31-4274. Metro: Intendente. Map p 75.*

Department Stores/ Shopping Centers
★★ Amoreiras Shopping
AMOREIRAS Opened in the 1980s and still the poshest of Lisbon's malls. With 219 stores, 50 restaurants, and 7 cinema screens all in an eye-catching postmodern decor (p 75). Look for international brands from Zara to Max Mara, plus a scattering of Portuguese designers. *Av. Eng. Duarte Pacheco. www. amoreiras.com,* ☎ *21/381-0200. Metro: Rato, Marquês de Pombal.*

★ Centro Colombo BENFICA
Once the largest shopping center in Europe, it boasts more than 420 retailers. You can buy everything from a Capt. America action figure to a 23,000€ white-gold-and-diamond engagement ring from local jeweler David Rosas. *Avenida Lusíada. www.colombo.pt.*

☎ *21/711-3600. Metro: Colégio Militar/Luz. See map p 75.*

★★ El Corte Inglés SÃO
SEBASTIÃO The classy Lisbon branch of this Spanish department store chain is a favorite with expats thanks to the international goodies in its basement supermarket. There are also 13 floors packed with upscale selections of fashion, perfumery, tech gadgets, and more. The many dining options range from tapas to gourmet restaurants. *Av. António Augusto de Aguiar, 31. www. elcorteingles.pt.* ☎ *70/721-1711 Metro: São Sebastião. Map p 75.*

★★★ Embaixada PRÍNCIPE
REAL A mall like no other. Housed in an Arabian Nights–style palace, it's an homage to Portuguese style, from eco-design furniture to organic cosmetics, fashionable footwear, and trendy updates of traditional mountain garb. Renowned restaurants, a gin bar hosting *fado* nights, and the city's sexiest staircase. *Praça do Príncipe Real, 26. www. embaixadalx.pt.* ☎ *96/530-9 154. Tram: 24. Map p 76.*

Selection of meat in El Corte Inglés department store.

Crafty Portugal

Portugal has a wealth of regional handicraft traditions. The small town of Arraiolos is famed for carpets. Hand-painted pottery from Coimbra is refined and colorful. Artists from Barcelos up north produce clay figures: demons, saints, and the rooster, which has become a national symbol. Delicate filigree jewelry is a specialty of Viana do Castelo. Madeira is famed for lacework. Ceramic tiles (*azulejos*) are central to Portuguese art, appearing on buildings ranging from ancient churches to brand-new subway stations.

Home Goods & Furnishings

★★ Casa dos Tapetes de Arraiolos PRÍNCIPE REAL   The little town of Arraiolos in the rolling Alentejo region south of Lisbon has a centuries-old tradition of weaving rugs from local wool. The intricate patterns are often inspired by the local flowers and influenced by Middle Eastern designs. The hand-sewn rugs sold here take months to make and don't come cheap, but you know they are genuine and not the Asian-made copies that have recently been appearing on the market. *Rua da Imprensa Nacional, 116E. www.casatapetesarraiolos.com.* ☎ *21/396-3354. Metro: Rato. Tram: 24. Map p 76.*

★ Cutipol CHIADO   A fusion of timeless skills and modern designs lies at the heart of this globally renowned Portuguese cutlery maker. The flagship store of this family-run business is a tableware treat. *Rua do Alecrim, 84. www.cutipol.pt.* ☎ *21/322-5075. Metro: Baixa-Chiado. Map p 77.*

★ 21PR Concept Store PRÍNCIPE REAL   This showroom for Portuguese and international creativity is a pleasingly cluttered space filled with art books, children's clothes, quirky art objects, and much else. A delight to browse. *Praça do Príncipe Real, 21.* ☎ *21/346-9421. Metro: Rato. Tram: 24. Map p 76.*

★★★ Vista Alegre CHIADO   A producer of fine porcelain since 1824, this gem of a shop in the heart of the Chiado elegantly displays its range of classic and contemporary designs. It works with leading chefs, artists, and designs to produce unique pieces. Also available: top-class crystal ware from the group's Atlantis factory. *Largo do Chiado, 20-23. www.vistaalegre.com.* ☎ *21/346-1401 Metro: Baixa-Chiado; Tram: 28. Map p 76.*

Fashion & Accessories

★★ A Outra Face da Lua BAIXA   A cave of vintage ranging from 1920s flapper dresses to '70s disco chic. Colorful and eccentric, the shop sells costume jewelry, hats, and handbags as well as clothes. The **built-in bar** is a popular downtown meeting place. *Rua da Assunção, 22. www.aoutrafacedalua.com.* ☎ *21/886-3430. Metro: Baixa-Chiado. Tram: 12,15, 25. Map p 77.*

★★★ Azevedo Rua BAIXA   Portugal's oldest hatter is little changed since the owner's grandfather opened it on Rossio Square in 1886. Kings of Spain, presidents of Portugal, and poet Fernando

Sardine tins from A Vida Portuguesa.

Pessoa got their head gear here. Aside from a head-spinning selection of hats and caps, there are some fine gentleman's canes. *Praça Dom Pedro IV, 72–73. www.azevedo rua.pt.* ☎ *21/342-7511. Metro: Rossio. Map p 76.*

★★ Kolovrat PRÍNCIPE REAL
Bosnian-born Lidija Kolovrat is Lisbon's designer of the moment. Her Príncipe Real boutique is alive with vivid shades and daring shapes for men and women. *Rua Dom Pedro V, 79. www.lidijakolovrat.com.* ☎ *21/ 387-4536. Tram: 24. Bus: 758. Map p 76.*

★★ Dama de Copas
BAIXA   Starting from the principle that 90% of women wear ill-fitting bras, two Polish immigrants created "Queen of Cups," offering personalized fitting and consulting service, plus an expanded range of sizes to ensure a perfect fit from A to K. The concept took off, and they now have lingerie stores across Portugal and Spain. *Rua de Santa Justa 87. www.damadecopas.com.* ☎ *21/195-5997. Metro: Rossio. Map p 76.*

★★ Pelcor PRÍNCIPE REAL
Portugal is the world's biggest producer of cork, and everything in this shop is made from the naturally produced bark. Choose from handbags to umbrellas, hats, and belts. *Pátio do Tijolo, 16.* ☎ *21/886-4205. Tram: 24. Map p 76.*

★★ Storytailors CHIADO
Designers João Branco and Luis Sanchez create clothes with theatrical flair beautifully shown over three floors of an 18th-century townhouse. Off-the-peg designs and a made-to-measure service popular with stars of stage and screen. *Calçada do Ferragial 8. www.story tailors.pt.* ☎ *21/343-2306. Tram: 25, 28. See map p 76.*

Gifts

★★ A Arte da Terra ALFAMA
Located in a historic building in the heart of Alfama, this store sells some of the best regional crafts, from embroidery to ceramics. *Rua de Augusto Rosa. www.aartedaterra. pt.* ☎ *21/274-5975. Tram: 28. Map p 77.*

★★★ A Vida Portuguesa
INTENDENTE   Created in 2007 to preserve and promote traditional Portuguese merchandise, today it has four stores in Lisbon that serve as a time capsule. The biggest

offers 6,000 authentic products from shepherds' blankets to cereals in 1930s boxes and trendy Bordalo Pinheiro ceramics. Smaller outlets are in Chiado and Time Out Market. *Largo do Intendente 23. www. avidaportuguesa.com.* ☎ *21/197-4512. Metro: Intendente. Map p 75.*

★★★ Caza das Vellas Loreto

CHIADO Opened in 1789, this is perhaps Lisbon's most beautiful shop. It sells aromatic handmade candles and feels like an intimate Gothic chapel, with arched wood panels and bundles of colored wax. *Rua Loreto 53/5. www.cazavellas loreto.com.pt.* ☎ *21/342-5387. Metro: Baixa-Chiado. Tram: 28. Map p 76.*

★★★ Claus Porto BAIRRO ALTO

This firm from the northern city of Porto has been making soaps and perfumes since 1887. It's renowned for its retro packaging and works with top perfumers making scents inspired by the Portuguese country-side. The store is a sensory delight. *Rua da Misericórdia, 135. www.claus porto.com.* ☎ *91/721-5855. Metro: Baixa-Chiado. Tram: 24. Map p 76.*

Artisanal meats in Manteigaria Silva.

Gourmet Food & Drink

★★ Conserveira de Lisboa

BAIXA Portugal is a canned-fish superpower, and this 1930s store is the place to stock up on a pungent piscatorial present. Tuna, sardine, anchovy, and squid are just some of the critters squeezed into the retro-style tins. *Rua dos Bacalhoeiros, 34. www.conserveiradelisboa.pt.* ☎ *21/886-4009. Metro: Terreiro do Paço. Tram: 28. Map p 77.*

★★ Garrafeira Nacional

BAIXA If you have 8,900€ to spare, pop in to buy a 1780 vintage Madeira. Thankfully, this wine store opened in 1927 has some more affordable bottles among the over 6,000 wines and spirits on offer. *Rua de Santa Justa, 18. www.garrafeira nacional.com.* ☎ *21/887-9080. Metro: Baixa-Chiado. Map p 76.*

★★★ Manteigaria Silva BAIXA

The aromas of salt cod, cured hams, and ripe cheese assail you as you enter this grocery, opened in 1890. It's a taste of old Lisbon. They take their food very seriously here, stocking artisan products from around the regions. *Rua Dom Antão de Almada, 1. www.manteigariasilva. pt.* ☎ *21/3 42-4905. Metro: Rossio. Map p 76.*

Jewelry

★★ Leitão & Irmão CHIADO

It's been almost 150 years since the Emperor of Brazil made these guys court jewelers, but they are still going strong, selling everything from traditional filigree to contemporary designs, from engagement rings to silver plates. Additional branches in Bairro Alto, Estoril, and the Four Seasons Hotel Ritz. *Largo do Chiado 16. www.leitao-irmao.com.* ☎ *21/325-7870. Metro: Baixa-Chiado. Tram: 28 Map p 76.*

★★ **Maria João Bahia** AVENIDA DE LIBERDADE Internationally renowned designer Bahia still takes inspiration from her Portuguese homeland. Her creations in sterling silver, pure gold, and quality gems are exhibited in this handsome, upscale boutique. *Av. da Liberdade 102. www.mariajoaobahia.pt.* ☎ *21/3 240 018. Metro: Avenida. Map p 75.*

Music

★★ **Discoteca Amália** BAIXA A great selection of *fado* recordings, from the late diva Amália Rodrigues to today's hot names like Gisela João, Raquel Tavares and Carminho. *Rua Aurea, 274.* ☎ *21/342-0939. Metro: Baixa-Chiado. Map p 76.*

★★ **Louie Louie** CHIADO A funky store with thousands of new and used vinyl and CD recordings. Rummage among a range running from jazz to punk, disco to *fado*. *Rua Nova da Trindade. www.louie louie.biz.* ☎ *21/347-2232. Metro: Baixa-Chiado. Map p 76.*

Shoes & Leather Goods

★★ **Cubanas** CHIADO Despite the name, these shoes for men and women are 100% Portuguese. The stylish-but-fun footwear is exported around the world, but the best place to buy it is right here. *Largo Rafael Bordalo Pinheiro, 31. A. www. cubanas-shoes.com.* ☎ *91/237-4516. Metro: Baixa-Chiado. Map p 76.*

★★★ **Fly London** AVENIDA DE LIBERDADE Portugal is second only to Italy as an exporter of quality footwear and this uber-trendy brand played a large role in establishing its reputation. Under the slogan "always progressive, never conventional," their shoes are sold in over 3,000 outlets from Greece to Greenwich village. It's hard to miss the store on Lisbon's poshest avenue: It has a giant bat over the door. *Av. da Liberdade, 230. www. flylondon.com.* ☎ *91/059-4 564. Metro: Avenida. Map p 75.*

★★★ **Luvaria Ulisses** CHIADO Opened in 1925, this tiny store selling leather gloves is one of the last surviving independent retailers on the Rua do Carmo. The service and the handmade gloves are of the finest quality. *Rua do Carmo, 87-A. www.luvariaulisses.com.* ☎ *21/342-0295. Metro: Rossio. Map p 76.*

★★★ **Luís Onofre** AVENIDA Michelle Obama and Paris Hilton have been spotted sporting shoes made by this Portuguese designer. A third-generation shoemaker, Onofre blends time-honored techniques and leading designs to create shoes that don't come cheap, but are a mark of distinction. *Avenida da Liberdade, 247. www.luis onofre.com.* ☎ *21/131-3629. Metro: Marquês de Pombal. Map p 75.* ●

Along **the Riverbanks**

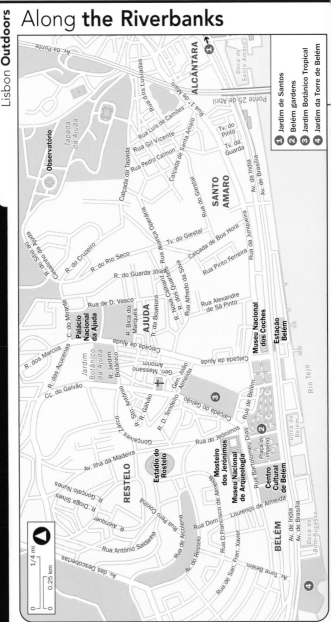

1 Jardim de Santos
2 Belém gardens
3 Jardim Botânico Tropical
4 Jardim da Torre de Belém

Previous page: Museum of Art, Architecture and Technology.

Lisbon used to turn its back to the river, with docks and warehouses cutting off the city from the Tagus. Now the riverbanks are lined with walkways, gardens, and cycle paths heading west from Praça do Comércio all the way to Belém and—with just a few breaks—onwards toward the beaches of Oeiras and Cascais. **Jardim dos Santos. Train: Santos. Metro: Cais do Sodré. Tram: 25. Bus: 706, 727, 774.**

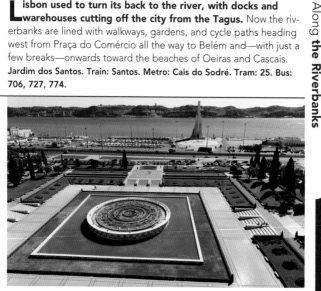

Empire Square, in the Praça do Imperio.

❶ ★ **Jardim de Santos.** This cozy urban garden makes a good starting point for a riverside stroll. After appreciating its dense vegetation, including the pink blooming Judas trees and a fine South American Tipuana tree, you can climb over the footbridge crossing the railway line heading to Cascais to find the walking and cycling paths heading west. *Largo de Santos. Admission free. Open daily 8am–8pm. Train: Santos. Metro: Cais do Sodré. Tram: 25. Bus: 706, 727, 774.*

❷ ★ **Belém gardens.** The 4-mile riverside walk from downtown to Belém passes working docks, warehouses converted into restaurants, lawns, and museums like the **Orient Foundation** (p 67) and **MAAT** (p 42). When you arrive, there are three interlinked gardens, on the landward side of the road and railway lines. This was the site of an ambitious exhibition in 1940 to celebrate Portugal's colonial empire—and the gardens carry reminders of that imperial age: the grand **Praça do Império** with its walkways, cypress trees and fountains; the towering monument to Afonso de Albuquerque, a 16th-century conqueror in Asia overlooking the formal gardens named for him; and the more laidback **Jardim Vasco da Gama,** whose lawns are popular for picnics. It has a surprising attraction: a brightly colored **Thai pavilion,** a 2012 gift from the Bangkok government to celebrate 500 years of diplomatic relations. *Avenida da Índia. Admission free. Open 24 hr. Train: Belém. Tram: 15. Bus: 706, 714, 727, 728, 729, 797, 751.*

❸ ★★ **Jardim Botânico Tropical.** Set up in 1902 as the Colonial Gardens for research into tropical agriculture, it's now a verdant escape from the crowds of Belém. The entrance is tucked away to the

The LX Factory: Riverfront Regeneration

The threads and fabrics industry that bustled along the riverfront in this sprawling brick barracks is long gone. What was once one of the city's most important industrial sites in Alcântara has been reborn as the **LX Factory,** a dynamic and charmingly rough-hewn arts center and multi-use complex of architecture and design firms, shops, cafes, fashion, and cultural happenings—you name it. The vaunted **Ler Devagar** bookshop has a gloriously huge, four-level space here in a former printworks. LX Factory shops have a sustainable-practices bent, from **Nae,** making vegan Portuguese shoes of cork and other eco-friendly microfibers, to **Amazingstore,** offering crafts made of wood and other sustainable materials. Add to that an organic cosmetics shop, an eco-home design store, wine shops, and numerous cool and cutting-edge restaurants and bars. It even has a **Sunday flea market,** where vendors sell vintage clothing and handmade crafts on the old cobblestones outside, and street art on practically every pockmarked surface of the old factory. Rua Rodrigues de Faria 103. www.lxfactory.com. ☎ **314-3399.** Opening times vary.

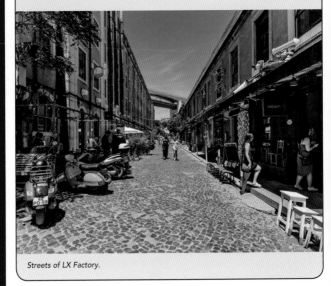

Streets of LX Factory.

Colorful Thai pavilion in Belém's Vasco da Gama garden.

side of **Jerónimos** monastery (p 14). There are over 17 acres planted with 600 species, mostly from Africa, Asia and the Americas. Highlights include majestic rows of Washingtonia palms, rare Chinese ginkos and Canary Island dragon trees. Run by Lisbon University, it still has a research role. There's an 18th-century mansion amid the forest that's used for exhibitions and colonial-era artworks including a Chinese archway from Macau and colonial-era statues representing African and Asian peoples. *Largo dos Jerónimos. www.museus.ulisboa. pt.* ☎ *21/392-1808. Admission 2€;*

Stone monoliths at the Champalimaud Centre for the Unknown.

1€ seniors and ages 12–18; free children 11 and under. Oct–Mar 9am–5pm; Apr–Sept 9am–8pm. Train: Belém. Tram: 15, 18. Bus: 714, 727, 728, 729

④ ★★ Jardim da Torre de Belém. Ten acres of lawns and palm trees from which to contemplate the white tower jutting into the river that is Lisbon's best-known landmark (p 14). The gardens contain a replica of the seaplane in which Carlos Gago Coutinho and Artur de Sacadura Cabral made the first flight across the South Atlantic in 1922. To the side is a moving memorial to soldiers killed in Portugal's Colonial Wars (1961–1975). It bears the names of 9,273 fallen. A next-door fort has a military museum. Take a short walk past the fort and you'll reach the startlingly modern structures of the Champalimaud Centre for the Unknown, built in 2010 by Indian architect Charles Correa. You can stroll the grounds of this state-of-the-art research center and relax in the excellent riverfront cafe/restaurant. (p 103). The gardens are the site of free jazz concerts in the summer. *Avenida de Brasília. Free entry. Open 24 hr. Train: Alges. Tram 15. Bus 729.*

City Center Gardens

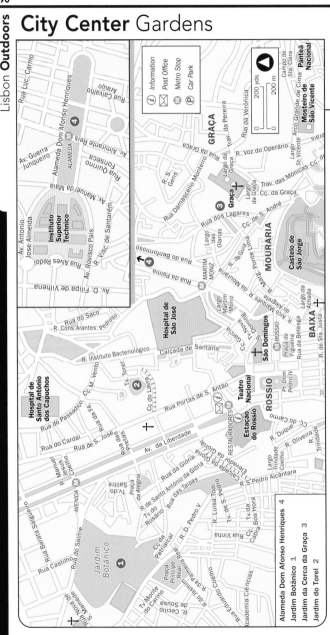

Information
Post Office
Metro Stop
Car Park

Alameda Dom Afonso Henriques	4
Jardim Botânico	1
Jardim da Cerca da Graça	3
Jardim do Torel	2

Lisbon has a wealth of urban parks and gardens where you can relax, smell the roses, and even play. The most well-known include the Parque Eduardo VII (p 20), the Gulbenkian gardens (p 19), and the Jardim da Estrella. But the the city offers even more worthy green spaces to explore, including an aromatic botanical garden that's a major attraction in its own right. START: Jardim da Estrela. Tram: 25, 28. Bus: 9, 720, 738, 773.

The tranquil Jardim Botânico.

1 ★★★ kids Jardim Botânico. A jungle of biodiversity in the heart of the city, Lisbon's botanical garden reopened in 2018 after an 18-month facelift. It clings to a hillside above Avenida da Liberdade, giving you glimpses of cross-town vistas as you wind through the vegetation. The gardens are home to more than 1,500 species, from towering palms to bamboo forests. Discover rare specimens like the *árvore-do-imperador* (emperor's tree), threatened with extinction in its native Brazil, or cycad plants, which have been around since the time of the dinosaurs. The gardens, first opened in 1878, are run by the neighboring **Natural History and Science Museum**, also well worth a visit. *Rua da Escola Politécnica 56/58. www.museus.ulisboa.pt.* ☎ *21/392-1800. Admission 3€; 1.50€ seniors and ages 10–18; free for children 9 and under. Daily Oct–Mar 9am–4:30pm; Apr–Sept 9am–7:30pm. Metro: Rato. Tram: 24. Bus: 758, 773.*

2 ★ kids Jardim do Torel. On the other side of Avenida da Liberdade—and with views across to the botanical garden—is this leafy hideaway. In August, locals don trunks and bikinis to join the mermaid statues in the large ornamental pond. Open-air movies are another summer diversion. The garden is ringed by mansions at the top of the Lavra funicular. *Rua Júlio de Andrade 46. Free admission. Daily 7am–10pm. Metro: Avenida. Bus: 760.*

3 ★ Jardim da Cerca da Graça. A new addition to Lisbon's green spaces opened in 2015 on the steep slope below Graça viewpoint. It has 4 acres of lawns, 180 newly planted trees, a kiosk café, a picnic area, and a playground. And, of course, great city views. *Calçada Do Monte 46. Free admission. Daily 10am–10pm. Tram: 28. Bus: 734.*

4 ★ kids Alameda Dom Afonso Henriques. Rows of trees and a broad lawn run for 700 yards down this boulevard leading to the shops of the Rua de Londres shopping street. At the top end is the Fonte Luminosa, a spectacular fountain built in the1940s' "New State" dictatorship style, complete with nymphs and muscular horsemen. Cost-cutting means the water isn't always turned on, but there are displays most afternoons and colored lights after sundown. *Alameda Dom Afonso Henriques. Metro: Alameda. Bus: 708, 713, 717, 720, 735, 736.*

West to **Monsanto**

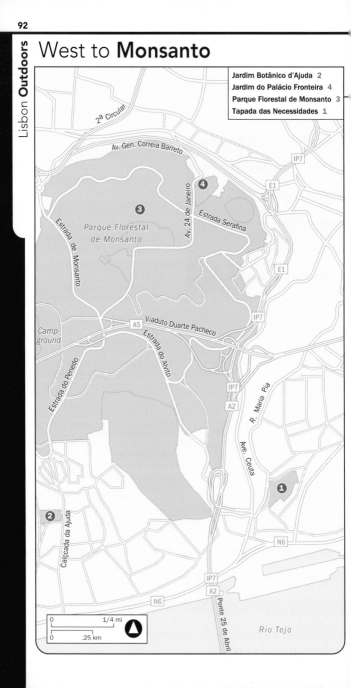

Jardim Botânico d'Ajuda 2
Jardim do Palácio Fronteira 4
Parque Florestal de Monsanto 3
Tapada das Necessidades 1

Vast, hilly Monsanto Forest Park is more than three times the size of New York's Central Park. It's Lisbon's lung, but just one of several worthy green spaces west of the city. This tour includes a palace garden and a former royal hunting grounds.

The ornamental Ajuda Garden.

❶ ★ Tapada das Necessidades. This secret garden is unknown even to many locals, yet it is said to have inspired one of the world's most famous paintings. French artist Édouard Manet wrote that his risqué Le Déjeuner sur l'herbe was painted after a visit to this bucolic garden in 1859. In earlier times, the garden was a hunting ground and picnic spot for the royal family. It lies just behind the pink-hued Palácio das Necessidades, a baroque royal palace that serves as Portugal's Foreign Ministry. The gardens are a bit rundown, especially the domed greenhouse, but still make a romantic hideaway. *Largo das Necessidades. Admission free. Oct–Mar Mon–Fri 8am–6pm, Sat–Sun 10am–6pm; Apr–Sept Mon–Fri 8am–7pm, Sat–Sun 10am–7pm. Train: Alcantara-Terra Bus: 712, 713, 727, 742, 773*

❷ ★ Jardim Botânico d'Ajuda. Breathe in the scents of exotic flora in Portugal's oldest botanic garden, planted in 1768 near Ajuda palace (p 68). It's a seasonal festival of color, with orchids, river views, and peacocks. The formal layout includes lakes, trimmed hedges, and a baroque fountain. *Calçada da Ajuda.* ☎ *21/362-2503. Admission 2€; 1€ seniors and students; free for children 6 and under. Nov–Mar 10am–5pm; Apr & Oct Mon–Fri 10am–5pm, Sat–Sun 10am–6pm; May–Sept Mon–Fri 10am–6pm, Sat–Sun 9am–8pm. Tram: 18. Bus: 727, 729, 732.*

Gardens at the Palacio dos Marquises de Fronteira.

Monsanto Viewpoint.

❸ ★★ kids Parque Florestal de Monsanto. Taking up 10 percent of the city area, Europe's largest urban woodland contains over 4 square miles of hilly land on the city's western edge. Monsanto is covered in natural wild vegetation, thick with oak and umbrella pine. Old and young alike come for the biking, hiking, and riding trails; adventure parks with ropeways through the trees; and picnic spots and playgrounds. *Information Estrada do Barcal, Monte das Perdizes.* ☎ *21/817-0200. Free admission. Open 24 hr. Bus: 711, 724, 770.*

❹ ★★★ Jardim do Palácio Fronteira. This is one of the world's 250 top gardens. Formally laid out among spectacular displays of *azulejos*, fountains, and statues on the edge of Monsanto forest. Descendants of the Marquis of Fronteira still live in the 17th-century palace, but it too can be visited on morning guided tours. *Largo de São Domingos de Benfica, 1. www.fronteira-alorna.pt.* ☎ *21/778-2023. Admission 4€. Oct–May Mon–Fri 11am–1pm and 2–7pm, Sat 11am–1pm; June–Sept Mon–Fri 10:30am–1pm and 2–5pm, Sat 10:30am–1pm. Tram: 15. Bus: 770.* ●

Dining Best Bets

Best for **Carnivores**
★★ Adega das Gravatas $
Travessa do Pregoeiro, 15e (p 101)

Best for **Sharing**
★★ Pharmacia $$$ *Rua Marechal Saldanha, 1 (p 107)*

Best **Riverside Location**
★★★ Monte Mar $$$$ *Rua da Cintura, Armazém, 65 (p 105)*

Best **Fine Dining**
★★★ Belcanto $$$$$ *Largo de São Carlos (p 101)*

Best **Seafood**
★★★ Ramiro $$$ *Avenida Almirante Reis, 1 (p 107)*

Best **Service**
★★★ Varanda de Lisboa $$$ *Praça Martim Moniz 2 (p.38)*

Best **Creative Cuisine**
★★★ 100 Maneiras $$$$ *Rua Teixeira, 35 (p 106)*

Best **Budget Dining**
★★ Casa dos Passarinhos $ *Rua Silva Carvalho, 195 (p 102)*

Best for **Traditional Portuguese**
★★★ Dom Feijão $$ *Largo Machado de Assis, 7D (p 103)*

Best **Tropical Cuisine**
★★ Ibo $$$$ *Armazém A Cais do Sodré (p 104)*

Best for **Hipsters**
★★★ Rio Maravilha $$$ *Rua Rodrigues Faria, 103 (p 108)*

Best for a **Tête-à-tête**
★★★ Estórias na Casa da Comida $$$$ *Travessa das Amoreiras, 1 (p 103)*

Best **City Views**
★★ The Insólito $$$ *Rua de São Pedro de Alcântara, 83 (p 108)*

Best for **Decor**
★★ Darwin's Café $$$ *Champalimaud Center for the Unknown, Av. Brasília (p 103).*

Above: Waterfront dining at Café In. Previous page: Dining on the patio of Rio Maravilha.

Alfama Dining

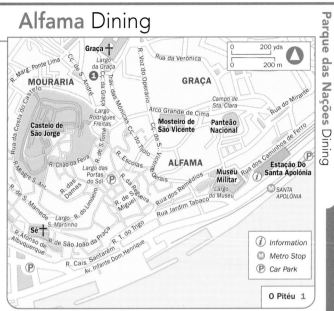

O Pitéu 1

Parque das Nações Dining

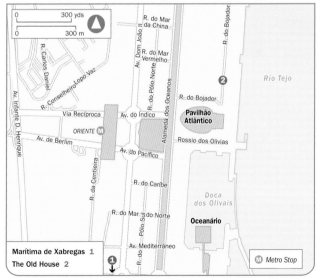

Marítima de Xabregas 1
The Old House 2

City Center Dining

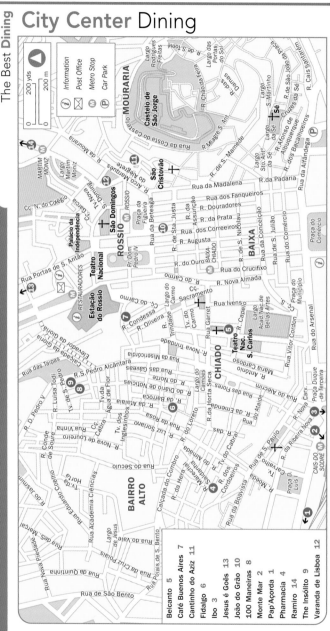

Information
Post Office
Metro Stop
Car Park

Belém Dining

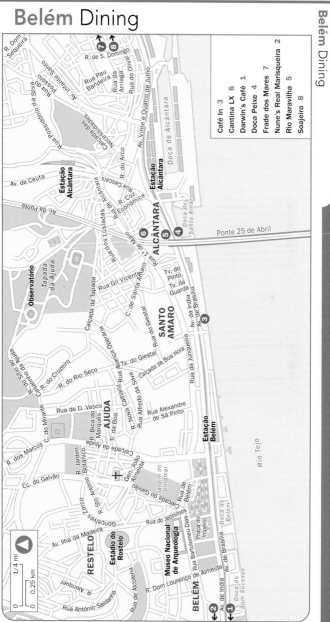

Café In 3
Cantina LX 6
Darwin's Café 1
Doca Peixe 4
Frade dos Mares 7
Nune's Real Marisqueira 2
Rio Maravilha 5
Soajeiro 8

North of City Center Dining

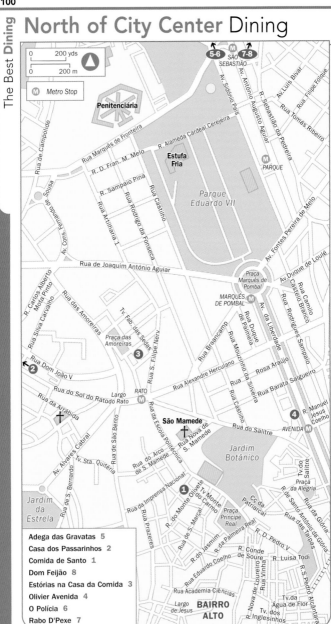

Adega das Gravatas **5**
Casa dos Passarinhos **2**
Comida de Santo **1**
Dom Feijão **8**
Estórias na Casa da Comida **3**
Olivier Avenida **4**
O Polícia **6**
Rabo D'Pexe **7**

Lisbon Dining A to Z

★★ Adega das Gravatas

CARNIDE *PORTUGUESE* The Carnide neighborhood has a quaint village-like feel, tucked away behind Benfica's stadium and the Colombo shopping mall. It's well off the beaten track but renowned among locals for traditional steak restaurants. This place was founded in 1908 and packs in crowds hungry for dishes like baked octopus soaked in olive oil and stone-cooked steak. It gets its name from the more than 3,000 neckties (*gravatas*) left by generations of customers who include many star names from the nearby soccer club. *Travessa do Pregoeiro, 15. www. adegadasgravatas.com.* ☎ *21/714-3622. Main courses 9.50€–18.50€. Closed Mon. Metro: Carnide. Map p 100.*

★★★ Belcanto CHIADO *MODERN PORTUGUESE*

As this book went to press, this was the only Lisbon restaurant with two Michelin stars. It's also ranked among the world's top 100. The centerpiece of chef José Avillez's empire of fine Lisbon eateries features an exclusive room of just 10 tables, across from the opera house. It offers a fabulously inventive take on Portuguese cuisine. Signature dishes on the six-course tasting menu include seabass with bivalves and algae, and suckling pig with orange. Book well in advance. *Largo de São Carlos, 10. www.belcanto.pt.* ☎ *21/342-0607. Main courses 49.50€–25€. Closed Sun and Mon. Metro Baixa/Chiado. Map p 98.*

★ Café Buenos Aires CHIADO *INTERNATIONAL*

The interior of this cafe, founded by an Argentine-Portuguese couple, resembles a cozy Parisian bistro. Lit by yellow street lamps, the terrace offers romantic views over the Baixa. Dishes reflect the owners' origins, like Argentine steak with chimichurri sauce or Portuguese salt cod in olive oil with sweet potatoes. It has occasional live tango nights. Fresh salads and pasta dishes make this a great stop for a light lunch too. *Calçada do Duque 31 B. www.cafebuenosaires. pt.* ☎ *21/342-0739. Main courses 11.50€–24€. No credit cards. Mon–Fri noon–1am; Sat–Sun 6pm–1am. Metro: Baixa/Chiado. Map p 98.*

★ Café In BELÉM *PORTUGUESE/ SEAFOOD*

This elegant riverside fish restaurant has sweeping views over the Tagus. The shellfish and charcoal-grilled fish (such as seabass or red mullet) are excellent. Ask for the catch of day. Like in many Portuguese restaurants, the fish is sold by the kilo, so choose the size you want. Popular at lunchtimes and at weekends, it can be quiet on weekday evenings. A relaxed lounge bar with an esplanade serves drinks and light meals. *Avenida Brasília, 311. www.cafein.pt.* ☎ *21/362-2249. Main courses 15€–25€. Open daily. Tram: 15. Map p 99.*

★ Cantina LX ALCÂNTARA

PORTUGUESE A canteen for print workers back when LX Factory was actually a factory rather than Lisbon's hippest post-industrial shopping, eating, and cultural hub. Cooking is traditional with the occasional twist—like coating a smoked *alheira* sausage in a sesame crust or adding lemon-basil sauce to the tuna steak. The decor is a homely junkyard jumble of recycled furniture and plastic table covers. *Lx Factory, R. Rodrigues*

Cantina LX.

Faria 103. www.cantinalx.com. ☎ 21/362 -8239. *Main courses 9.50€–16.50€. Open daily. Tram: 15. Map p 99.*

★ **Cantinho do Aziz** MOURARIA *MOZAMBICAN* Backstreet, family-run restaurant serving up the exotically delicious cuisine of Mozambique, a coconut- and chili-infused blend of African, Indian, and Portuguese flavors. Try crab curry; shrimp with okra; or baby goat with toasted coconut. Go easy on the iced 2M beers shipped in from southern Africa, chef Jeny's fiery piri-piri sauce, and the sweet cashew fruit mousse. *Rua de S. Lourenço 5. www.cantinhodoaziz.com. ☎ 21/887-6472. Main courses 8€–17€. Open daily. Metro: Martim Moniz. Map p 98.*

★★ **Casa dos Passarinhos** CAMPO DE OURIQUE *PORTUGUESE* It's increasingly hard to find places like this, simple neighborhood taverns known as *tascas*, serving home-style food to families and groups of friends according to time-honored recipes. This "house of little birds" is one of the best.

The menu changes daily; ask the white-shirted waiters for recommendations. Dishes include creamy monkfish rice with shrimp or grilled mackerel with cilantro and roe. It's handily located if you're visiting the Amoreiras shopping mall. *Rua Silva Carvalho 195. www.casados passarinhos.com. ☎ 21/388-2346. Main courses 9€–18.50€. Closed Sun. Metro: Rato. Bus: 758. Map p 100.*

★ **Comida de Santo** PRÍNCIPE REAL *BRAZILIAN* From your first drop of caipirinha to the last spoonful of papaya purée, this is a tropical adventure for the taste buds. One of Lisbon's oldest Brazilian restaurants, it gets its inspiration from the cooking of Salvador da Bahia, famed for its use of coconut, lime, and delicate spices. Typical dishes include *vatapá*, made with fish palm oil and cashew nuts and dried shrimp; or cured beef with cassava and *catupiry* cheese. *Calçada Engenheiro Miguel Pais, 39. www.comidadesanto.pt. ☎ 21/396-3339. Main courses 10€–18€. Closed Tues. Dinner only in Aug. Metro: Rato. Bus: 758/730. Map p 100.*

Abóbora recheada com camarão at Comida de Santo.

★★ **Darwin's Café** BELÉM
INTERNATIONAL With a spectacular waterfront location inside the
Champalimaud Center for the
Unknown, a cutting-edge science
center and architectural landmark,
this vast white space is dominated
by evolutionary-inspired modern
art. Mediterranean and Portuguese
influences mingle on a menu that
includes the likes of rabbit and red
wine risotto and salt cod under a
cornbread crust. *Champalimaud
Center for the Unknown, Av. Brasília.*
www.darwincafe.com. ☎ *21/048-
0222. Main courses 15.50€–26.50€.
Open daily; lunch only Mon. Tram:
15. Map p 99.*

★★ **Doca Peixe** ALCÂNTARA
PORTUGUESE/SEAFOOD This is
the pick of a row of restaurants in
converted dockside warehouses
right under the iconic April 25
Bridge. The freshest fish is expertly
chargrilled or oven-baked under a
salt crust. Jaw-dropping river views.
Doca de Santo Amaro, Armazém 14.
☎ *21/397-4790. Main courses*
*10€–16€. Open daily. Train: Alcântara
Mar. Tram: 15. Map p 99.*

★★★ **Dom Feijão** ALVALADE
PORTUGUESE Hallowed ground
for lovers of true Portuguese cuisine. Local families often besiege
this retro, open-plan dining room
off the Avenida de Roma shopping
street, so book in advance. Like
many in this mid-20th-century
neighborhood it's rooted in the
robust cooking of northern Portugal, serving baked turbot or roast
young goat. No one is quite sure
how it got its name, which translates as "Sir Bean." *Largo Machado
de Assis, 7D.* ☎ *21/846-4038. Main
courses 10€–17€. Closed Sun. Metro:
Roma. Map p 100.*

★★★ **Estórias na Casa da
Comida** AMOREIRAS *MODERN
PORTUGUESE* Occupying the
ground floor of an old townhouse
off one of Lisbon's must atmospheric squares, this joint oozes
old-world charm and has been a
standout on the Lisbon restaurant
scene for 40 years. It's built around
a courtyard garden and decorated

The Best Dining

The charming restaurant and bar of Casa da Comida.

with ceramics tiles and French Empire furnishings. Chef João Pereira's creations include black-belly rosefish with corn-broth and razor clams, or peasant stuffed with quince. *Travessa das Amoreiras, 1. www.casadacomida.pt.* ☎ *21/386-0889. Main courses 23€–30€. Dinner only; closed Sun. Metro: Rato. Map p 100.*

★ **Fidalgo** BAIRRO ALTO
PORTUGUESE With its marble-clad walls and displays of standout Portuguese wines, Fidalgo is a class apart from the tourist traps and cheap-booze joints that have infested much of the Bairro Alto. The cuisine is classical Portuguese. Daily specials may include rare treats like rice with salted cod cheeks or chargrilled boar. *Rua da Barroca 27.* ☎ *21/342-2900. Main courses 10€–17.50€. Closed Sun. Metro: Baixa-Chiado. Map p 98.*

★ **Frade dos Mares** SANTOS
PORTUGUESE/SEAFOOD Book early for a table at this cozy modern bistro which has built up a solid reputation among locals and visitors with its consistently excellent, mostly seafood dishes. Specialties include roast codfish and octopus with sweet potato. *Av. Dom Carlos I, 55. www.fradedosmares.com.* ☎ *21/390-9418. Main courses 15.50€–21€. Open daily. Tram: 25. Map p 99.*

★★ **Ibo** CAIS DO SODRÉ
MOZAMBICAN This is upscale Mozambican cooking with prices to match, but this former salt

Sampler of dishes at Ibo restaurant.

warehouse enjoys a prime riverside perch where you can watch the come and go of Tagus boats as you tuck into Indian Ocean cuisine. Start with crab and mango salad, move on to shrimp curry with okra, and finish up with papaya stuffed with ewe's-milk cream cheese. The owners also have a Portuguese-style seafood restaurant and a cafe serving craft ice cream next door. *Armazém A Cais do Sordé.* ☎ 96-133-2024. *Main courses 19€–33€. Closed Mon; lunch only Sun. Metro: Cais do Sordé. Map p 98.*

★ **Jesus é Goês** AVENIDA DA LIBERDADE *GOAN* Culinary exchanges between India and Portugal have been producing delicious results for 500 years—and nowhere more fruitfully than in the state of Goa, a Portuguese outpost until the 1960s. Chef Jesus Lee recreates the tropical charm and tangy flavors of his homeland in this brightly colored shrine to gastronomic intermingling. Try hot and sour baby shark or spiced cilantro chicken. On no account should you miss the date-filled samosas with ginger and cardamom ice cream. *Rua de São José, 23.* ☎ 21/154-5812. *Main courses 9€–20€. Closed Sun and Mon. Metro: Restauradores. Map p 98.*

★ **João do Grão** BAIXA *PORTUGUESE* Take care dining in the Baixa district. While good traditional restaurants survive, there are plenty of rip-off joints with hidden charges and substandard food. This place, whose name translates as "Johnny Chick Pea," is the real deal. In fact, it's been serving good, honest Portuguese food for well over 100 years. An ever-changing menu features seasonal specialties, but many locals come for the famed salt-cod (*bacalhau*) dishes. *Rua dos Correeiros 222. www.joaograo.pai.pt.* ☎ 21/342-4757.

8.50€–16€. *Open daily. Metro: Rossio. Map p 98.*

★★ **Marítima de Xabregas** XABREGAS *PORTUGUESE* Since 1966 families have been gathering in this warehouse-size dining space tucked away in the docklands between downtown and the Parque das Nações. Huge charcoal-fired grills are constantly filled with steak on the bone or slabs of codfish to be served with smoky skin-on potatoes. The more adventurous can try eel stew, a specialty along the Tagus. Portions are big; sharing is okay. *Rua Manutenção, 40. www.restaurantemaritimadexabregas.com.pt.* ☎ 21/868-2235. *Main courses 9.50€–18.50€. Closed Sat. Bus: 728/759. Map p 97.*

★★ **Monte Mar** CAIS DO SORDÉ *PORTUGUESE/SEAFOOD* In summer, diners flock to the deck of this fish restaurant, which juts out over the river Tagus. This is the little sister of a famed seashore spot in Cascais and shares its reputation for serving the freshest Atlantic seafood in a stylish waterfront setting. Much sought after is the fried hake with cockle rice. *Rua da Cintura, Armazém 65. www.mmlisboa.pt.* ☎ 21/322-0160. *Main courses 16.50€–30.75€. Closed Mon. Metro: Cais do Sordé. Map p 98.*

★★ **Nune's Real Marisqueira** BELÉM *PORTUGUESE/SEAFOOD* One of the best-known fish restaurants in the city, this bustling venue serves up superlative shellfish alongside grouper, John Dory, and turbot. The steaks are justly famed, but seafood is the main attraction. *Rua Bartolomeu Dias 120. www.nunesmarisqueira.pt.* ☎ 21/301-9899. *Main courses 17€–27€. Closed Mon. Tram: 15. Map p 99.*

★★ **Olivier Avenida** AVENIDA DA LIBERDADE *MEDITERRANEAN* Chef Olivier is a pioneer in Lisbon's

Bacalhau espuma das onda (cod stew) at 100 Maneiras.

food revolution, blending classical French techniques with fresh local produce. His flagship restaurant continues to pull in a glamorous crowd (a former prime minister, several ambassadors, and a scattering of *telenovela* stars were on show last time we visited). The food is a sophisticated fusion of French, Italian, and Portuguese, creating dishes like scallops gratin with truffle and duck *magret* in port wine. *Rua Júlio César Machado, 7. www. restaurantesolivier.com.* ☎ *21/317-4105. Main courses 18€–50€. Dinner only Sat; closed Sun. Metro: Avenida. Map p 100.*

★★★ **100 Maneiras** BAIRRO ALTO *MODERN PORTUGUESE* Yugoslav-born Chef Ljubomir Stanisic is a star in Portugal. He judges TV cooking contests, fronts food documentaries, and plays Gordon Ramsey's role in Portugal's own "Kitchen Nightmares." He's also a very good chef. The tasting menu at his relaxed-but-chic restaurant is a sensorial voyage of discovery. Creative combos include pig's foot

with kimchi and avocado, or oyster foam with passionfruit. At press time, the restaurant was moving two doors down (Rua do Teixeira, 39) and creating an "updated version" of 100 Maneiras—one that includes a vegetarian tasting menu. *Rua do Teixeira, 35. www.100 maneiras.com.* ☎ *91-091-8181. 10-course tasting menu 60€. Open daily. Tram: 24. Map p 98.*

★ **O Pitéu GRAÇA** *PORTUGUESE* Run by the same family since the 1960s, this is your typical neighborhood restaurant: decorative tiles on white walls, paper tablecloths, soccer game on the TV. It buzzes with the chatter of regular customers and curious newcomers wandering in from the nearby terminus of Tram 28. There's a wide daily range of traditional Portuguese dishes, but for many the highlight is fried fish served with tomato rice. *Largo da Graça, 95-96. www.restaurante opiteu.pt.* ☎ *21/887-1067. Main courses 8€–18€. Lunch only Sat; closed Sun. Tram: 28. Map p 97.*

★★ **O Polícia** AVENIDAS NOVAS *PORTUGUESE* Named for the ex-cop who founded it in 1900, this discreet little gem has a decor and menu that seems little changed in decades. The classic Portuguese food is consistently good, but you're in for a special treat if baked porgy (*pargo no forno*) is on the specials board. Close to the Gulbenkian Museum, it's popular for business lunches. *Rua Marquês Sá da Bandeira, 112A. www. restauranteopolicia.com.* ☎ *21/796-3505. Main courses 12.50€–19.50€. Lunch only Sat; closed Sun. Metro: São Sebastião. Map p 100.*

★★ **Pap'Açorda** CAIS DO SODRÉ *PORTUGUESE* Dodge the crowds at the Time Out Market food hall and head upstairs to this airy space on the first floor of the old market building. Hip since the 1980s (when it was based in the Bairro Alto), it serves topnotch Portuguese dishes with a dash of innovation. Winners include seafood rice and paprika-spiced black pork tenderloin. *Avenida 24 de Julho 49. www.papacorda.com.* ☎ *21/346-4811. Main courses 13€–36€. Closed Mon. Metro: Cais do Sodré. Map p 98.*

★★ **Pharmacia** BICA *MODERN PORTUGUESE* Chef Susana Felicidade shares her building with the pharmacy museum, and her restaurant has a medically inspired theme, serving cocktails with names like "ibuprofen" and "morphine." Don't let that put you off. The building is a lemon-colored hilltop palace with lawns and spectacular river views. Felicidade specializes in *petiscos* (Portuguese tapas) for sharing, like quail and partridge salad or catch-of-the-day fish stew. Be prepared to wait for an outside table at busy times. *Rua Marechal Saldanha, 1.* ☎ *21/ 346 2146. Main courses 9.80€–15.90€. Open daily. Metro: Baixa-Chiado. Tram 28. Map p 98.*

★★ **Rabo D'Pexe** SALDANHA *AZOREAN* Portugal's mid-Atlantic Azores islands are renowned for wonderful seafood and free-range beef. This place serves it up, flying in 80% of its fish and meat from the archipelago. Fish takes pride of place. Choose from the spectacular array of species on the ice tray, then watch chefs prepare it in the open kitchen. In addition to traditional Portuguese preparations, expert sushi chefs are on hand if you want it raw. Dishes are beautifully presented in a light-filled interior garden. *Avenida Duque de Ávila 42B.* ☎ *21/314-1605. Main courses 13€–17€. Open daily. Metro: Saldanha. Map p 100.*

★★★ **Ramiro** INTENDENTE *PORTUGUESE/SEAFOOD* This place has been popular since it was opened by a Spanish immigrant in the 1950s, but ever since the late Anthony Bourdain raved about it on TV, lines have stretched down the street. It's noisy, crowded, and chaotic, but the wondrous seafood makes it all worthwhile. The usual routine is to order a series of shellfish plates: clams with garlic and

Grilling fresh seafood at Ramiro.

Colorful cocktail at Rio Maravilha.

cilantro, say, or grilled giant shrimp or leathery goose barnacles. Wash it down with chilled beer or *vinho verde* and follow up with a steak sandwich. Try to find space for the fresh mango. They don't take phone reservations, so to avoid the queues, eat early (or late). *Avenida Almirante Reis,1. www.cervejaria ramiro.pt.* ☎ *21/885-1024. Seafood sold by weight; expect to pay 11€– 25€ for a 250g portion. Closed Mon. Metro: Intendente: 15. Map p 98.*

★★★ **Rio Maravilha** ALCÂN-TARA *INTERNATIONAL* A climb to the top floor of what was an old factory leads to this uber-trendy post-industrial space. It has expansive views over the river and some of the city's most interesting food. An innovative blend of Portuguese and Brazilian influences produces dishes like leg of lamb with peanut sauce or salt cod with caramelized turnips and miso. Sharing is encouraged. There's a happening bar outside restaurant hours. *Rua Rodrigues Faria, 103.* ☎ *96-602-8229. Main courses 16€–27€. Closed Mon; dinner only Tues; lunch only Sun. Tram: 15. Map p 99.*

★ **Soajeiro** SANTOS *MADEIRAN* This hole-in-the-wall does a range of Portuguese standards, but the lunchtime crowds are drawn by one dish: *espetada*. A specialty from the owner's Madeira island home, It comprises cubes of garlic-infused beef skewered on laurel branches, then grilled over hot coals. Get there early to avoid the lines, and try a *poncha*, the potent island cocktail. *Rua do Merca-Tudo, 16.* ☎ *21/397-5316. Main courses 7.50€–11€. Lunch only; closed Sun. Tram: 25. Map p 99.*

★★ **The Insólito** BAIRRO ALTO *MODERN PORTUGUESE* Location is the winner for this quirky restaurant and cocktail bar perched on the roof of a palatial hilltop townhouse. The views over the city are gorgeous. Choose from a list of inventive cocktails and more than 50 wines. The creative Portuguese cooking includes dishes like braised oxtail or chocolate tart with sour cherry sorbet and port wine. It can get noisy, and service can be slow at busy times. *Rua de São Pedro de Alcântara 83. www.theinsolito.pt.* ☎ *21/130-3306. Main courses 16€– 30€. Open daily dinner only. Tram: 24. Map p 98.*

★★ **The Old House** PARQUE DAS NAÇÕES *CHINESE* Lisbon has become a popular European base for wealthy Chinese, with the happy consequence that the number of very good Chinese restaurants has grown. The top-class Sichuan cuisine here is served in a stylish dining room and on a shady riverside terrace. The vast menu features dishes hard to find in Europe, like tea shrimp or chicken with Chinese yam. Appropriately, its address translates as "pepper street." *Rua Pimenta 9. www.theold houseportugal.pt.* ☎ *21/896-9075. Main courses 9.90€–45€. Open daily. Metro: Oriente: 15. Map p 97.* ●

Nightlife Best Bets

Best Port
★ Solar do Vinho do Porto,
Rua de São Pedro de Alcântara, 45
(p 121)

Best Vagabond Fado
★★★ Tasca do Chico, *Rua do*
Diàrio de Notícias, 39 (p 119)

Best Cocktails
★★ Cinco Lounge, *Rua Rubén A*
Leitao (p 113)

Best Gay Club
★★ Trumps, *Rua da Imprensa*
Nacional, 104B (p 121)

Best Posh Fado
★★ Senhor Vinho, *Rua do Meio à*
Lapa, 18 (p 119)

Best Interior
Pavilhão Chinês, *Rua Dom*
Pedro V, 89/91 (p 114)

Best Place for Dance Music
★★ Lux, *Avenida Dom Henrique*
(p 117)

Best Jazz
★★ Hot Clube de Portugal,
Rua da Alegría, 39 (p 121)

Best Rooftop Bar
★★★ Topo, *Centro Comercial*
Martim Moniz, Piso 6, Praça do
Martim Moniz (p 116)

Best Wine Bar
★★★ Vestigius, *Rua da Cintura*
do Porto de Lisboa, Armazém A, 17
(p 122)

Above: Pensão Amor. Previous page: Pavo Bar.

Alcântara/Belém Nightlife

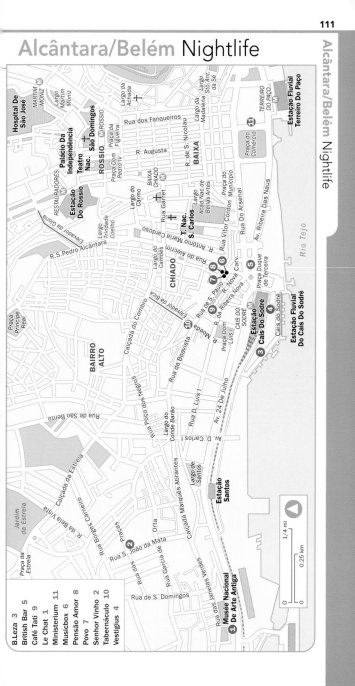

B.Leza 3
British Bar 5
Café Tati 9
Le Chat 1
Ministerium 11
Musicbox 6
Pensão Amor 8
Povo 7
Senhor Vinho 2
Tabernáculo 10
Vestígius 4

City Center Nightlife

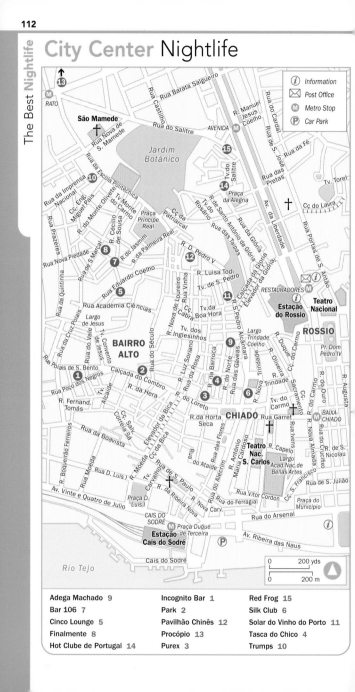

Parque das Nações Nightlife

A Baiuca 2
Casino Lisboa 6
Clube de Fado 1
Lux Frágil 5
Mesa de Frades 4
Topo 3

Lisbon Nightlife A to Z

Bars & Pubs

★ **British Bar** CAIS DO SODRÉ
This survivor started serving up
beer to British sailors in 1919 and
thrived when the Cais do Sodré was
a notorious rendezvous for ships'
crews and ladies of the night.
Although the area has since
become Lisbon's hippest nightlife
hub, the BB's dockside pub ambience is little changed. It serves up
an international selection of beer to
curious newcomers, seasoned
locals, and the bohemian types
who have always frequented it. The
pub starred in the cult 1980s movie
Dans la Ville Blanche. Try a refresh-
ing draft ginger beer and look for

the surreal timepiece behind the
bar. *Rua Bernardino Costa, 52.*
☎ *21/342-2367. Daily noon–4am.
Metro: Cais do Sodré. Map p 111.*

★★ **Cinco Lounge** PRÍNCIPE
REAL   Rated by many as Lisbon's
best cocktail bar, Cinco Lounge
was founded in 2005 by renowned
British mixologist Dave Palethorpe
with the aim of restoring "the lost
art of polite drinking." It's chic and
sophisticated but relaxed, and
renowned for its fiendishly inventive
cocktails—like the Sherlock Tones,
a blend of Scotch, apple juice, and
coconut ice cream, or the Hot Tub,
with Pampero rum, Grand Marnier,
orange, and cinnamon. *Rua Ruben*

Fado: Music for the Soul

Fado is to Lisbon what tango is to Buenos Aires or blues is to Chicago, an earthy urban music that is deeply engrained in the soul of the city. *Fado* grew out of the Lisbon docklands, heartfelt guitar-backed laments and bawdy ballads crooned by sailors, crooks, and ladies of the night. Its first star, Maria Severa (1820–1846), was a girl from the mean streets who was courted by bull-fighting nobility. In no time, fado took off among the aristocracy. In its classic form, fado features a solo singer backed by a classic guitar and a 12-string Portuguese *guitarra*. Radio, recordings, and movies gave fado respectability—and superstar **Amália Rodrigues** (1920–1999) (p 20) took it to a global audience. You can hear fado in posh *casas de fado* over expensive dinners, in taverns where cooks and waiters belt out tunes, and in concert halls where a new generation of singers like Mariza, Gisela João, and Ana Moura (who has sung with the Rolling Stones) draws thousands of fans. Although most think of fado as songs of sadness belted out by black-clad women, the music can be up-tempo and funny. Some of its biggest stars are male, like Camané and Grammy winner Carlos do Carmo. Lisbon's best fado joints are much sought after by foreign visitors. As a general rule, the later you go, the more they fill up with Portuguese aficionados.

A. Leitão, 17A. www.cincolounge. com. ☎ 21/342-4033. Daily 9pm–2am. Tram: 24. Map p 112.

★ **Le Chat** SANTOS   A glass cube and open terrace perched on a clifftop overlooking the River Tagus next to the Museum of Ancient Art, Le Chat is a cool place to relax after perusing the paintings. Sip *caipirinhas* late into the night as boat lights twinkle in the water. It serves light meals, craft beers, and a selection of wines and classic cocktails. *Jardim 9 de Abril.* ☎ 21/396-3668. Mon–Sat 12:30pm–2am; Sun 12:30pm–midnight. Bus: 713, 714, 727. Map p 111.

★★ **Park** BAIRRO ALTO   A little hard to find given that it's on the roof of six-story carpark on the edge of the hilltop Bairro Alto district, Park rewards with extraordinary views. Deck chairs and potted plants give it a chilled, garden feel. Park has burgers, R&B sets, and a signature cocktail combining gin with *ginja*—a Portuguese sour cherry liqueur. It can get crowded, especially around sunset. No reservations. *Calçada do Combro, 58, Piso 6.* ☎ 21/591-4011. Mon–Sat 1pm–2am. Tram: 28. Map p 112.

★★★ **Pavilhão Chinês** PRÍNCIPE REAL   This is like stepping into a labyrinthine Victorian curiosity cabinet. Walls are lined with bric-a-brac: regiments of lead soldiers, shoals of ceramic sea creatures, busts of long-departed European aristocracy. One of the discreetly lit salons is filled with military headgear;

another has flights of vintage model aircraft. Opened in 1986 in a 100-year-old grocery store, the "Chinese pavilion" is like an eccentric gentleman's club, complete with billiards room. The drinks list is an inch thick. *Rua Dom Pedro V, 89/91.* ☎ *21/342-4729. Daily 6pm–2am. Tram: 24. Map p 112.*

★★★ **Pensão Amor** CAIS DO SODRÉ With its decadent air of an Edwardian bordello, this hip bar recalls Cais do Sodré's shady past—although the real brothels here were never this fancy. The crimson interior is laden with erotic artworks. There are crystal chandeliers and velvet sofas, shimmering curtains, and quiet side rooms suggestive of intimate encounters. It's laidback during the day but heats up after dark with an eclectic program that can include burlesque shows, live jazz, funky DJ sessions, or literary *tertulias. Rua do Alecrim, 19. www.pensaoamor.pt.* ☎ *21/314-3399. Sun–Wed 2pm–3am;*

Thurs–Sat 2pm–4am. Metro: Cais do Sodré. Map p 111.

★ **Procópio** AMOREIRAS Charming little place with a 1920s feel hidden in a back street next to the lovely Jardim das Amoreiras. Its plush, Art Nouveau interior and bluesy soundtrack make it perfect for a quiet drink or one of their famed toasted sandwiches. *Alto de S. Francisco, 21. www.barprocopio. com.* ☎ *21/385-2851. Mon–Fri 6pm–3am; Sat 9pm–3am. Metro: Rato. Map p 112.*

★★ **Red Frog** AVENIDA DA LIBERDADE With its New York speakeasy vibe, the Red Frog in 2017 became the first Portuguese joint to make it onto the prestigious World's 100 Best Bars list. It's renowned for its astonishingly beautiful cocktails, presented more like works of art than booze. Like the Guilty Latin Boys, a mix of Venezuelan rum, guava, raw cocoa, and lime and decorated with more flowers and fruit than a Carmen Miranda

Bartender at Bar Procopio Amoreiras.

Colorful fountain show at the Casino Estoril.

headdress; or the Fat Duck, with 12-year-old single malt, Portuguese muscatel wine, cranberries, and slices of duck breast. Like all good speakeasies, the door is locked; buzz to enter. *Rua do Salitre, 5A. www.redfrog.pt.* ☎ *21/583-1120 Mon–Thurs 6pm–2am; Fri–Sat 6pm–3am Metro: Avenida. Map p 112.*

★★★ **Topo** MARTIM MONIZ One of Lisbon's hippest rooftops sits atop a rather gloomy shopping mall filled with Chinese textile stores and an excellent Indian grocer in Lisbon's most multicultural neighborhood. Topo has proved so successful that it's spawned a couple of offshoots in more tony parts

Performance in the Arena Lounge at Casino Lisboa.

of the city, but this remains the most atmospheric. Hot music, great views of St. George's Castle, *petiscos* (small dishes) that reflect the area's diversity, and an intoxicating mix of classic and creative cocktails. *Centro Comercial Martim Moniz, Piso 6, Praça do Martim Moniz. ☎ 21/588-1322. Sun–Thurs 12:30pm–midnight. Fri–Sat 12:30pm–2am. Metro: Martim Moniz. Map p 113.*

Casinos

★ **Casino Lisboa** PARQUE DAS NAÇÕES Estoril's smaller sister is closer to the city in the modern, riverside Parque das Nações district. It offers many of the same attractions including blackjack, baccarat, and poker tournaments. Top-class *fado* singers sometimes perform at the casino's theater. *Alameda dos Oceanos. ☎ 21/466-7700. Metro: Oriente. Map p 113.*

★★ **Estoril Casino** ESTORIL Europe's largest casino has changed a bit since a young British intelligence officer named Ian Fleming visited during WWII, finding inspiration for his first James Bond novel *Casino Royale*. Still, it remains Lisbon's most glitzy nightspot, with vast gaming rooms, 1,110 slot machines, bars, dance floors, and international stars performing onstage. Just a short walk from the beach in the resort suburb of Estoril, the casino is owned by Macau gaming magnate Stanley Ho, who installed the **Mandarim** restaurant here, considered one of the best places in Europe for Cantonese food. *Avenida Dr. Stanley Ho, Estoril. ☎ 21/466-7700. Daily 3pm–3am. Train: Estoril.*

Dance Clubs

★★★ **B.Leza** CAIS DO SODRÉ This legendary club is the place to dance to Angolan *kizomba*, Cape

Verdean *funaná*, and other sensual rhythms from Portuguese-speaking Africa. Opened in the 1990s in a dilapidated palace, it relocated in 2012 to a renovated quayside warehouse. The surroundings are more modern, but the energy levels from the DJs and live bands are unabated. Musicians from other musical styles from samba and *fado* to reggae often appear. Improve your moves with the regular Sunday dance classes. *Cais da Ribeira Nova, Armazém B. ☎ 21/010 6837. Wed–Thurs 10:30pm–4am; Fri–Sat 10:30pm–5am; Sun 6pm–2am. Metro: Cais do Sodré. Map p 111.*

★★★ **Lux Frágil** SANTA APOLÓNIA Lisbon's hottest club lists John Malkovich among its founders, and his Hollywood A-list buddies have been seen to shake their stuff here. Occupying a former warehouse overlooking the Tagus, it has a laid-back upstairs bar, outdoor terrace, and a river-level

Ana Marta performing at Timpanas.

dance floor where some of the world's top DJ's lay down a frenetic beat. Its reputation means you'll need to be early or famous to make sure you get in. *Avenida Infante Dom Henrique, Armazém A. www. luxfragil.com.* ☎ *21/882-08 90. Thurs–Sun 11pm–6am. Metro: Santa Apolónia. Map p 113.*

★ **Ministerium** BAIXA   In the heart of the city, this club took over part of the Ministry of Finance in 2012. The 18th-century building was built to withstand earthquakes so has no problem dealing with throbbing all-night techno. Aside from the regular Saturday opening hours, check its Facebook page for frequent special events. *Praça do Comércio, 72.* ☎ *21/888-8454. Sat 11pm–6am. Metro: Terreiro do Paço. Map p 111.*

★★ **Silk Club** CHIADO   Perhaps the city's most exclusive club. Located on the top floor of a seven-story Chiado mansion, it's the place to sip champagne, gulp designer sashimi, and watch the sunset—the rooftop views are stunning. As the night progresses, and particularly on weekends, things heat up with DJs spinning dance sets into the wee small hours. They operate a bottle service and it's wise to book ahead. *Rua da Misericórdia, 14.* ☎ *91-193-7740. Tues–Wed 7pm–1am; Thurs 7pm–1:30am; Fri–Sat 7pm–4pm. Metro: Baixa-Chiado. Map p 112.*

Fado

★ **A Baiuca** ALFAMA   This is for *fado vadio*—vagabond fado, which means the singers are amateurs singing for the enjoyment of it. The quality of the singing, food, and service can be mixed, but the atmosphere is always special and the guitarists excellent. Squeeze around one of the tiny tavern's

Guitar at Clube de Fado.

communal tables, order up some simple food and red wine, and sit back as the waiters, cook, and various neighbors step up to sing. Expect to be hissed if you talk during the performance. *20 Rua de São Miguel.* ☎ *21/886-7284. Thurs–Mon 8pm–midnight. Tram: 12, 28. Map p 113.*

★★ **Adega Machado** BAIRRO ALTO   With its distinctive tiled facade showing musical scenes, this has been a Bairro Alto landmark since 1937. It's a classy place for dinner with live *fado* under the artistic direction of leading guitarist and singer Marco Rodrigues. As with most top *fado* houses, the food is expensive (mains 30€–35€), but this is a place with real tradition, where Amália once sang and European royalty listened. A good initiation is the "fado in the box" sessions featuring an hour of music and snacks daily at 5pm. The owners have two other houses, the

Café Luso nearby and **Timpanas** in Alcântara. *Rua do Norte, 9. www. adegamachado.pt.* ☎ *21/342-2282. Daily 7:30pm–2am. Tram: 24. Map p 112.*

★★ Clube de Fado ALFAMA Founded by virtuoso *fado* guitarist and composer Mario Pacheco and in a prime location behind the cathedral, this is a top-quality venue. Pacheco himself often plays, joined by famed singers like Cuca Roseta and Maria Ane Bobone. The food (mains 23€–33€) sometimes struggles to match the music, but this is one of the places where the *fado* stars (not to mention the likes of Woody Allen and Cristiano Ronaldo) come to listen to *fado. Rua São João da Praça, 86-94. www. clube-de-fado.com.* ☎ *21/885-2704. Daily 8pm–2am. Tram: 12, 28. Map p 113.*

★★ Mesa de Frades ALFAMA Another place beloved by *fado* insiders, this was opened in 2006 by guitarist Pedro Castro in a chapel lined with beautiful 18th-century *azulejos* (painted wall tiles). You'll need to book in advance to secure a table for dinner (mains 13€–18€), but many people squeeze in to enjoy the singing and drink standing up late at night, when if you're lucky you'll catch some of *fado*'s biggest names popping in for an impromptu jam session. *Rua dos Remédios, 139A.* ☎ *91-702-9436. Daily 8pm–2:30am. Metro: Santa Apolónia. Map p 113.*

★★ Povo CAIS DO SODRÉ This youthful "artistic tavern" stands out among the rowdy nightlife spots of Cais do Sondré's notorious "pink street." From Tuesday to Sunday 8pm to 10pm, it showcases young *fado* singers who rotate in for 3-month residencies. Let the music serenade you while you tuck into the menu of *petiscos* (snacks), from tempura green beans (5.50€) to shrimp in garlic (15€). There are late-night DJ sets. On Monday evenings, Povo hosts poetry readings. *Rua Nova do Carvalho, 32. www. povolisboa.com.* ☎ *21/347-3403. Sun–Wed 6pm–2am; Thurs–Sat 6pm–4am. Metro: Cais do Sodré. Map p 111.*

★★ Senhor Vinho LAPA This *casa do fado* opened in 1975 by renowned singer Maria da Fé. The rustic-chic decor and groups of besuited diplomats and business types among the diners recall bygone times. The biggest draw is Aldina Duarte, one of today's best *fado* voices, along with other excellent up-and-coming *fadistas*. Food is rigorously traditional with mains around 30€. Singing starts at 9pm. *Rua do Meio à Lapa, 18. www. srvinho.com.* ☎ *21/397-2681. Mon–Sat 8pm–2am. Bus: 713, 773. Map p 111.*

★★★ Tasca do Chico BAIRRO ALTO Revered ground for *fado* fans. As the photos covering the walls show, just about anybody who's anybody in contemporary *fado* has stood up and opened their lungs here. Serving snacks, sandwiches, and jugs of wine (the flame-grilled sausages are famed), this simple tavern showcases *fado vadio* at its best. It gets packed most evenings, especially since the late Anthony Bourdain gave it his seal of approval on international TV. Go late to increase your chances of seeing a big-name star drop in. A second branch is in Alfama. *Rua do Diàrio de Notícias, 39.* ☎ *96-133-9696. Sun–Thurs 7pm–1:30am; Fri–Sat 7pm–3am. Metro: Baixa-Chiado. Map p 112.*

Jazz

★★ Café Tati CAIS DO SODRÉ Tucked away behind the busy Ribeira market, Tati is a laidback

Musicians at Hot Clube de Portugal.

cafe where neighborhood folk gather for coffee, wine, or a light meal amid the vintage furniture and art-covered walls. Its regular jam sessions on Tuesdays, Sundays, and occasionally other evenings are a magnet for jazz fans. Eurovision Song contest winner Salvador Sobral started his career here and still drops by for the occasional croon. *Rua da Ribeira nova, 36.* ☎ *21/346-1279. Tues–Sun 11am–1am. Metro: Cais do Sodré. Map p 111.*

★★★ Hot Clube de Portugal
AVENIDA DE LIBERDADE This classic jazz cellar is one of Europe's oldest clubs, bopping since the 1940s. According to legend, the youthful founders would grab musicians off planes that in those days stopped over between Paris and New York. It runs a renowned school for musicians and is still the capital's coolest joint. *Praça da Alegria, 48. www.hcp.pt.* ☎ *21/346-0305. Tues–Sat 10pm–2am. Metro: Avenida. Map p 112.*

★★Tabernáculo CAIS DO SODRÉ
Hernâni Miguel is feted as the father of Lisbon nightlife. His latest venture is a chilled-out bar serving fine wines under the cave-like arches of a centuries-old townhouse. The bar is decorated with covers of vintage soul, blues, and jazz albums, and live jazz is offered on Sunday and Friday. Other evenings, the bar hosts poetry readings, art exhibitions, and the occasional African food night. *Rua de São Paulo, 218.* ☎ *91-944-8385. Daily 2:30pm–2am. Metro: Cais do Sodré. Map p 111.*

LGBT Bars/Clubs
★ Bar 106 PRÍNCIPE REAL
A small, unassuming gay bar behind a closed door in the city's most popular gay neighborhood. Now entering its third decade, it also hosts parties and theme nights and is particularly lively on Sunday during its "message parties." Mixed ages and nationalities. *Rua de São Marçal, 106.* ☎ *21/342-7373. Mon–Thurs 9pm–2am; Fri–Sun 9pm–3am. Tram: 24. Map p 112.*

★★ Finalmente PRÍNCIPE REAL Celebrating its 40th anniversary in 2018, Finalmente is famed for its 3am drag shows starring Lisbon legend Deborah Krystall. The place many people end up at after a long night is also one of the city's most popular for cruising. *Rua da Palmeira 38. www.finalmenteclub.com.* ☎ *21/347-9923. Daily midnight–6am. Bus 773. Map p 112.*

★★ Purex BAIRRO ALTO One of the most popular bars among lesbians, Purex is renowned for its eclectic decor, electronic dance music (on a snug dance floor), and the mixologist's superlative Cosmopolitans. *Rua das Salgadeiras, 28.* ☎ *21/342-1942. Sun–Thurs 10pm–2am; Fri–Sat 10pm–3am. Metro: Baixa-Chiado. Map p 112.*

★★★ Trumps PRÍNCIPE REAL Long Lisbon's hottest gay venue, Trumps has a cafe, bars, and a dance club spread over two floors.

Performers at Trumps.

The decor is a mix of metal, glitter, and neon lighting downstairs, black floors and trendy chandeliers upstairs. The music is pop/house, with regular performances showcasing everything from flamethrowers to drag acts. *Rua da Imprensa Nacional, 104B. www.trumps.pt.* ☎ *91-593-8266. Metro: Rato. Map p 112.*

Rock

★★ Incognito Bar BAIRRO ALTO A stronghold of indie, new wave, and alternative rock since the 1980s. It lives up to its name: An unmarked door leads to the dance floor, where the club's dedicated followers will be grooving beneath the array of glitter balls. *Rua Poiais de São Bento, 37.* ☎ *21/390-8755. Wed–Sat 11pm–4am. Tram: 28. Map p 112.*

★★ Musicbox CAIS DO SODRÉ Featuring international and Portuguese bands alternating with DJ sets, Musicbox is a cultural icon for Lisbon nighthawks. It's renowned for rock, but the diverse programming ranges from house and funk to African and Brazilian beats. Everything happens in a cavern-like space under a much-Instagramed archway. *Rua Nova do Carvalho, 24. www.musicboxlisboa.com.* ☎ *21/347-3188. Daily 11pm–6am. Metro: Cais do Sodré. Map p 111.*

Wine Bars

★ Solar do Vinho do Porto BAIRRO ALTO This comfortable bar in an 18th-century palace is a good place to relax at the end of a day's sightseeing. Sink into a sofa and sample from the selection of port wines—the bar has more than 300 to choose from, and you can take a bottle home if you taste something you fancy. Prices vary enormously, but you don't have to spend a fortune to get something

The breezy patio at Vestigius.

palatable. Service needs an upgrade. *Rua de São Pedro de Alcântara, 45.* ☎ *21/347-5707. Mon–Fri 11am–midnight. Tram: 24. Map p 112.*

★★★**Vestigius** CAIS DO SODRÉ More than 1,000 wines are available for tasting in this warehouse whose terrace is lapped by the waters of the Tagus. It also has some 40 types of gin, cocktails, and light meals. The interior is artfully shabby-chic, designed by owner Esmeralda Fetahu. Staff is friendly and knowledgeable. It's an ideal spot for watching the little ferry-boats criss-cross the river. *Rua da Cintura do Porto de Lisboa, Armazém A, 17. www.vestigius.pt.* ☎ *30-880-4861. Sun–Thurs 11am–11pm; Fri–Sat 11–12:30am. Tram: 15. Map p 111.* ●

Advance Tickets & Listings

You can pick up the city's monthly "Agenda Cultural Lisboa" at hotels, museums, and tourist offices, or go online (www.agenda lx.pt). An alternative is **"Follow Me Lisboa,"** produced by the tourist office (www.visitlisboa.com). The Portuguese site of *Time Out* magazine (www.timeout.pt) also has listings of cultural events. You can buy tickets from online booking services such as **TicketLine** (www.ticketline.pt) and **BOL** (www.bol.pt) or from **FNAC stores** or the **FNAC website** (bilheteira.fnac.pt). One important thing to remember: Unlike in many European countries, Portugal generally shows movies in their original language, with subtitles, rather than dubbing Hollywood into the local lingo.

Arts & Entertainment Best Bets

Best **Concert Acoustics**
★★★ Fundação Calouste Gulbenkian, *Avenida de Berna (p 128)*

Best **Opera House**
★★★ Teatro Nacional de São Carlos, *Rua de Serpa Pinto (p 128)*

Best for **Contemporary Performance Arts**
★★★ Centro Cultural de Belém, *Praça do Império (p 127)*

Best **Ballet Venue**
★★★ Teatro Camões, *Passeio do Neptuno (p 128)*

Best **Sporting Event**
★★★ SL Benfica, *Avenida Eusébio da Silva Ferreira (p 130)*

Best **Theater Performances**
★★ Teatro Nacional Dona Maria II, *Praça Dom Pedro IV (p 130)*

Best for **Musicals**
★★ Teatro Politeama, *Rua das Portas de Santo Antão (p 130)*

Best for **International Superstars**
★★ Altice Arena, *Rossio dos Olivais (p 127)*

Best **Neighborhood Moviehouse**
★★ Cinema City Alvalade, *Avenida de Roma (p 128)*

Best **Moviehouse for Festivals**
★★ Cinema de São Jorge, *Avenida da Liberdade (p 129)*

Best **Moviehouse for Classic Films**
★★★ Cinemateca, *Rua Barata Salgueiro (p 129)*

Best for **Theater in English**
★★ The Lisbon Players, *Rua da Estrela (p 130)*

Above: Atlantico Pavilion. Previous page: Valentino Rossi in Circuito Estoril.

Campo Pequeno Arts & Entertainment

Campo Pequeno	6
Cinema City Alvalade	8
Culturgest	5
Gulbenkian Música	4
Medeia Monumental	2
SL Benfica	3
Sporting Clube de Portugal	7
UCI El Corte Inglés	1

Belém Arts & Entertainment

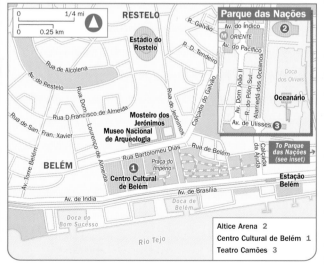

Altice Arena	2
Centro Cultural de Belém	1
Teatro Camões	3

City Center Arts & Entertainment

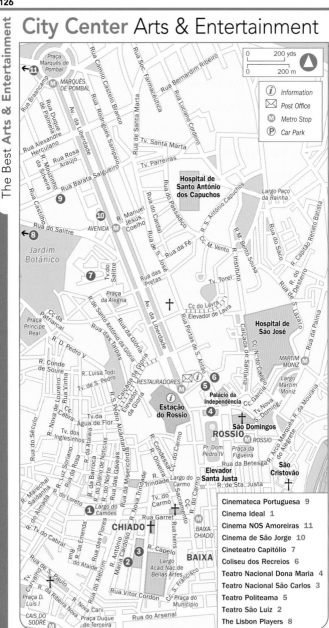

| 0 | 200 yds |
| 0 | 200 m |

ⓘ Information
✉ Post Office
Ⓜ Metro Stop
Ⓟ Car Park

Cinemateca Portuguesa 9
Cinema Ideal 1
Cinema NOS Amoreiras 11
Cinema de São Jorge 10
Cineteatro Capitólio 7
Coliseu dos Recreios 6
Teatro Nacional Dona Maria 4
Teatro Nacional São Carlos 3
Teatro Politeama 5
Teatro São Luiz 2
The Lisbon Players 8

Arts & Entertainment **A to Z**

Classical Music & Concert Venues

★★ Altice Arena PARQUE DAS NAÇÕES
Holding 20,000 spectators under its spaceship-like dome, this is one of Europe's biggest indoor music venues. It was built for the 1998 World Fair in the riverside Parque das Nações district and is the venue of choice for A-list stars passing through Lisbon. *Rossio dos Olivais. www.arena.altice.pt.* ☎ *21/891-8409. Metro: Oriente. Map p 125.*

★★★ Centro Cultural de Belém BELÉM
As well as holding one of Lisbon's foremost modern art collections (p 43), the vast CCB holds a performing-arts center with two auditoriums boasting excellent acoustics. The world-class program features classic music, jazz, *fado*, plus theater and contemporary dance performances. *Praça do Imperio. www.ccb.pt.* ☎ *21/361-2697. Train: Belém. Tram: 15. Map p 125.*

★★ Cineteatro Capitólio AVENIDA DA LIBERDADE
Recently restored to its former glory, this 1930s Art Deco landmark hosts an eclectic program of Portuguese and international acts from hip hop to flamenco, indie rock to standup comedy. *Parque Mayer. www.capitolio.pt.* ☎ *21/138-5340. Metro: Avenida. Map p 126.*

A stage at Centro Cultural de Belém.

★★ Coliseu dos Recreios
AVENIDA DA LIBERDADE   This historic venue dates back to the late 19th century, when it was the concert and show destination. Its striped dome catches the eye from many of Lisbon's *miradouros*. Holding up to 4,000 spectators, it's a cherished center for popular culture, hosting performances by musicians ranging from Patti Smith to the London Symphony Orchestra. Selling out the Coliseu is the ultimate sign of recognition for Portugal's *fado* stars. *Rua das Portas de Santo Antão. www. coliseulisboa.com.* ☎ *21/324-0585. Metro: Restauradores. Map p 126.*

Performance at the Coliseu dos Recreios.

Cellists in the Gulbenkian Orchestra.

★★★ Gulbenkian Música AVE-NIDAS NOVAS

The Gulbenkian center has first-class concert facilities as well as art collections (p 32). The foundation's choir and orchestra frequently play with international star performers. Although the focus is on classical music, regular shows feature jazz and folk musicians from around the world. Operas beamed in live from the Met in New York are a popular attraction. In summer, alfresco performances are held in the wonderful gardens. *Avenida de Berna, 45A. www.gulbenkian.pt.* ☎ *21/782-3461. Metro: São Sebastião, Praça de Espanha. Map p 125*

Opera and Dance

★★ Culturgest CAMPO PEQUENO

Run by one of Portugal's biggest banks, this multi-arts venue hosts a variety of cutting-edge music, theater, and art shows. *Rua Arco do Cego, 50. www.culturgest.pt.* ☎ *21/790-5454. Metro: Campo Pequeno. Map p 125.*

Performance at Culturgest.

★★★ Teatro Camões PARQUE DAS NACOES

Another legacy of the 1998 World's Fair, this riverside stone-and-glass theater is home to the Companhia Nacional de Bailado (National Ballet Company). The CNB's repertoire ranges from classical to contemporary ballet, but it has built its reputation around groundbreaking modern dance. *Passeio Neptuno. www.cnb.pt.* ☎ *21/892-3477. Metro: Oriente.*

★★★ Teatro Nacional de São Carlos CHIADO

Lisbon's grand opera house was built after the 1755 earthquake. It boasts a grand neoclassical facade and a sumptuous rococo interior (p 63). The opera season usually runs from October through May, and it's wise to book tickets in advance. The São Carlos is also the home to the **Orquesta Sinfónica Portuguesa,** whose full concert program runs through fall and winter. *Rua Serpa Pinto, 9. www.tnsc.pt.* ☎ *21/325-3045. Metro: Baixa-Chiado. Tram: 28. Map p 126.*

Film

★★ Cinema City Alvalade ALVALADE

This charming neighborhood movie house has a nice mix of Hollywood blockbusters and European films on its four screens. The cool bar/cafe out front is decorated with a 1950s mural depicting artistic endeavors and antique film posters showing how movies were promoted before they moved to shopping-mall

multiplexes. *Avenida de Roma, 100. www.cinemacity.pt.* ☎ *21/841-3043. Metro: Alvalade. Map p 125.*

★★ Cinema de São Jorge AVE-
NIDA DA LIBERDADE   This was the biggest cinema in Portugal when it opened in 1950. Today, it's the last survivor of the grand old movie houses along Avenida da Liberdade. It's used for premieres, festivals, and other events. *Avenida da Liberdade, 174. www.cinemasaojorge.pt.* ☎ *21/ 310-3400. Metro: Avenida. Map p 126.*

★★ Cinema Ideal CHIADO
Portugal's oldest cinema opened in 1904, but after lying abandoned for years, it reopened as the only regular movie house in the city's historic center. It mostly shows European arthouse movies, which is challenging if you can't read Portuguese subtitles, but when English-language films are playing, this is undoubtedly the coolest hangout for cinephiles. *Rua do Loreto, 15-17. www.cinema ideal.pt.* ☎ *21/099-8295. Metro: Baixa-Chiado; Tram 28. Map p 126.*

★ Cinema NOS Amoreiras
AMOREIRAS   This comfortable multiplex in Lisbon's snazziest shopping mall (p 80) mostly shows the latest Hollywood releases, plus a scattering of Portuguese and French films. *Amoreiras Shopping, Avenida Engenheiro Duarte Pacheco. www.cinemas. nos.pt.* ☎ *16996. Metro: Rato, Marquês de Pombal. Bus: 713, 758, 774. Map p 126.*

★★★ Cinemateca Portuguesa
AVENIDA DA LIBERDADE   More than just a cinema, this is a museum, archive, exhibition center, and bookshop, all housed in a palatial 19th-century building. It shows three or four films a day on the two screens. A typical bill could include a British sci-fi flick from the 1950s, a Pacino/De Niro doubleheader, and a French costume drama. On summer evenings, it's great to have

Vintage projector equipment in the Cinema de São Jorge.

pre-movie drink or meal in the rooftop bar. *Rua Barata Salgueiro, 39. www.cinemateca.pt.* ☎ *21/359-6262. Metro: Avenida. Map p 126.*

★★ Medeia Monumental
SALDANHA   Apart from showing an excellent mix of movies, from the latest blockbusters to vintage classics, this little theater also has a bar serving a wide range of Belgian and German beers and some of the best burgers in town. *Avenida Praia da Vitória, 72. www.medeiafilmes.com.* ☎ *21/314-2223. Metro: Saldanha. Map p 125.*

★ UCI El Corte Inglés SÃO
SEBASTIÃO   This multiplex in the basement of a swish Spanish department store (p 80) is the biggest in town, boasting 14 screens showing the latest releases. *Avenida Antonio Augusta Aguiar. www.ucicinemas.pt. Metro: São Sebastião. Map p 125.*

Spectator Sports
★★ Campo Pequeno CAMPO
PEQUENO   The home of Portuguese bullfighting holds *corridas* from April through October (p 168). The fights here are very different from those in Spain, comprising a

Bullfighters in the Campo Pequeno.

first part on horseback and a second where teams of men attempt to wrestle the bull to a standstill with their bare hands. Unlike in Spain, bulls are not killed in the ring, but many Portuguese who still view the sport as cruel call for a ban. *Centro de Lazer Campo Pequeno. www. campopequeno.com.* ☎ *21/799-8450. Metro: Campo Pequeno. Map p 125.*

★ **Circuito Estoril** ESTORIL The last Formula 1 Grand Prix was held back in the 1990s, but speed freaks can still get a thrill at the storied track watching auto and motorbike racing and classic car events at the circuit. *Av. Alfredo César Torres, Alcabideche. www.circuito-estoril.pt.* ☎ *21/460-9500. Bus: Est.*

★★★ **SL Benfica** BENFICA Portugal is soccer-crazy, and Benfica is its biggest club (despite what fans of Sporting might tell you) and a two-time European champion. Home games are packed with atmosphere, especially if Benfica is playing Sporting or northern upstarts FC Porto. The **Estádio de Luz stadium** (p 33) holds 65,000, but you'll still need to book in advance for big games. The club has teams playing basketball, track, and two dozen other sports. *Av. Eusébio da Silva Ferreira. www. slbenfica.pt.* ☎ *21/721-9500. Metro: Colégio-Militar/Luz. Map p 125.*

★★ **Sporting Clube de Portugal** CAMPO GRANDE Nicknamed the Lisbon Lions, Sporting is the crosstown rival to the Eagles of Benfica. At press time, they hadn't won the title in 16 years. It's still the club that nurtured the young Cristiano Ronaldo, and its fans make home games every bit as fervent as Benfica's. *Estádio José Alvalade, Rua Professor Fernando da Fonseca. www. sporting.pt.* ☎ *707-204-444. Metro: Campo Grande. Map p 125.*

Theater

★★ **The Lisbon Players** ESTRELA The show has gone on for Lisbon's English-language theater group since 1947. It's still putting on superior amateur performances that range from French farce to David Mamet. *Estrela Hall, Rua da Estrela, 2. www.lisbonplayers.com.pt.* ☎ *21/396-1946. Metro: Rato. Tram: 28, 25.*

★★ **Teatro Nacional Dona Maria II** BAIXA Portugal's national theater presents quality drama in a grand 19th-century playhouse (p 61). Almost all plays are in Portuguese without subtitles. *Praça D. Pedro IV. www.tndm.pt.* ☎ *21/325-0835. Metro: Rossio. Map p 126.*

★★ **Teatro Politeama** BAIXA This pretty downtown theater opened in 1912 and was famously the scene of a brawl between Nazi and Allied supporters when *Casablanca* had its Portuguese premiere here during WWII. Today, it's the realm of Lisbon's musical-comedy king, Filipe La Féria. *Rua das Portas de Santo Antão, 109. www.filipelaferia.pt.* ☎ *21/340-5700. Metro: Restauradores. Map p 126.*

★★ **Teatro São Luiz** CHIADO One of Lisbon's grandest theaters, opened in the 1890s, showcases dance, theater, and music. *Rua António Maria Cardoso, 38. www. teatrosaoluiz.pt.* ☎ *21/325-7640. Metro: Baixa-Chiado. Map p 126.* ●

Lodging Best Bets

Best **Historic Hotel**
★★ Avenida Palace $$$ *Rua 1° de Dezembro, 123 (p 138)*

Best **Boutique Hotel**
★★★ As Janelas Verdes $$$ *Rua das Janelas Verdes, 47 (p 138)*

Best **Modern Hotel**
★★★ Myriad by SANA Hotels Lisboa $$$$ *Rua das Cais das Naus (p 142)*

Best **City Center Location**
★★★ Pousada de Lisboa $$$$ *Praça do Comércio, 31-34 (p 144)*

Best for **Luxury**
★★★ Palácio Belmonte $$$$$ *Páteo Dom Fradique, 14 (p 143)*

Best **Views**
★★★ Memmo Alfama $$$ *Travessa Merceeiras, 27 (p 142)*

Best **Hideaway**
★★★ As Janelas Verdes $$$ *Rua das Janelas Verdes, 47 (p 138)*

Best for **Tranquility**
★★ Hotel da Estrela $$$ *Rua Saraiva de Carvalho, 356 (p 140)*

Best **Hostel**
★★ Sunset Destination Hostel $ *Praça do Duque de Terceira (p 145)*

Best **Palace Hotel**
★★★ Pestana Palace Hotel $$$$ *Rua Jau, 54 (p 144)*

Best for **Families**
★★★ Martinhal Lisbon Chiado Family Suites $$$$ *Rua das Flores, 44 (p 142)*

Best **Facilities**
★★★ Four Seasons Hotel Ritz $$$$$ *Rua Rodrigo da Fonseca, 88 (p 139)*

Best **on a Budget**
★★ Hotel Convento do Salvador $$. *Rua do Salvador, 2B (p 140)*

Best **Spa Pampering**
★★★ Altis Belém $$$$ *Doca de Bom Sucesso (p 138)*

Above: Salon at Casa do Barão. Previous page: Alberto Caeiro suite at Palacio Belmonte.

Belém/Alcântara Lodging

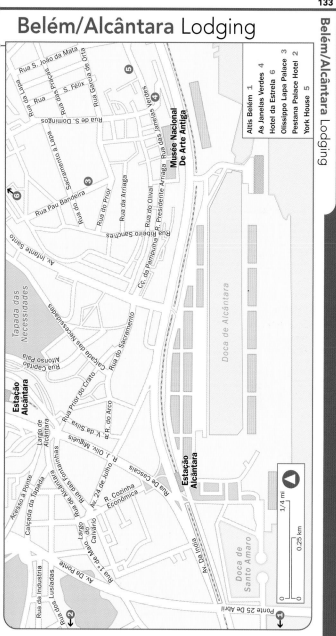

Altis Belém 1
As Janelas Verdes 4
Hotel da Estrela 6
Olissippo Lapa Palace 3
Pestana Palace Hotel 2
York House 5

Parque das Nações Lodging

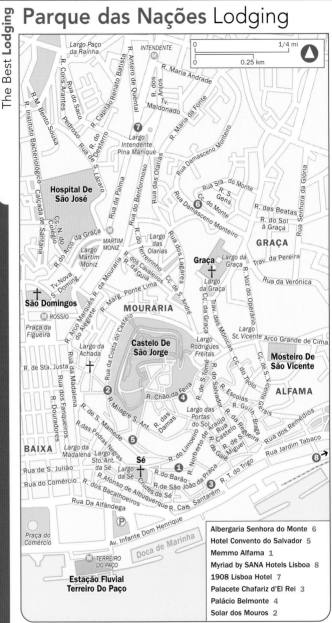

Albergaria Senhora do Monte 6
Hotel Convento do Salvador 5
Memmo Alfama 1
Myriad by SANA Hotels Lisboa 8
1908 Lisboa Hotel 7
Palacete Chafariz d'El Rei 3
Palácio Belmonte 4
Solar dos Mouros 2

North of Center Lodging

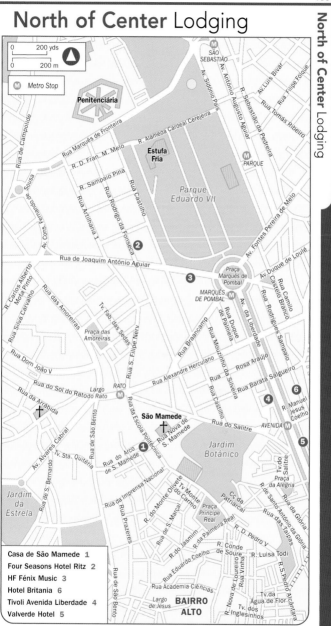

Casa de São Mamede 1
Four Seasons Hotel Ritz 2
HF Fénix Music 3
Hotel Britania 6
Tivoli Avenida Liberdade 4
Valverde Hotel 5

City Center Lodging

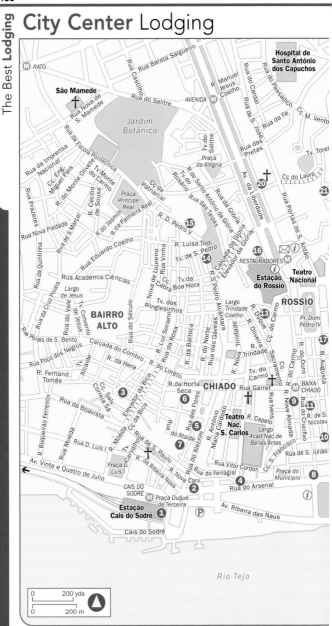

Information

Post Office

Metro Stop

Car Park

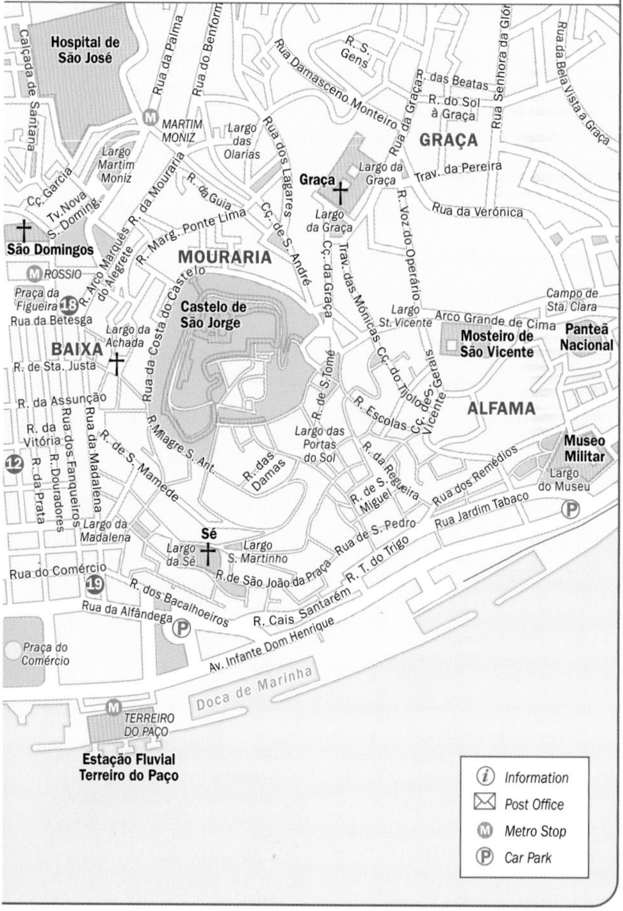

Lisbon Lodging A to Z

★ **Albergaria Senhora do Monte** GRAÇA   It's off the beaten track, a bit dated, and with rooms on the small side, but the bedroom views in this little place are among the best in town. Perched on a hilltop in an old neighborhood served by Tram 28, the inn makes a fine budget option. The best rooms have balconies and big windows overlooking the city and river. All guests can enjoy the vistas from the top-floor breakfast room. *Calçada do Monte, 39.* ☎ *21/886-6002. 26 units. Doubles 110€–150€. Tram: 28. Map p 134.*

★★★ **Altis Belém** BELÉM   Opened in 2009, this cool white cube of modernist luxury is so close to the waterfront it feels like a cruise liner floating down the River Tagus. Rooms are spacious and airy with Discoveries-inspired decor, river views, and natural light pouring in. Perfectly located to take in Belém's World Heritage attractions, it has a rooftop pool, one of the city's best spas and the Michelin-starred **Feitoria** restaurant. *Doca de Bom Successo. www.altishotels.com.* ☎ *21/040-0200. 55 units. Doubles 152€–523€. Tram: 15. Map p 133.*

★★★ **As Janelas Verdes** SANTOS   This boutique hotel in an 18th-century mansion was home to the novelist José Maria Eça de Queiros, whose 19th-century epic *The Maias* is set nearby. Designer Graça Viterbo has given it a comfortably contemporary feel in keeping with the literary history. Rooms have modern facilities and period charm. The mansion's ivy-clad garden is the place for breakfast with river views. The masterpieces of the Museu de Arte Antiga are just next door. *Rua das Janelas Verdes, 47. www.asjanelasverdes.com.*

☎ *21/396-8143. 29 units. Doubles 144€–441€. Tram: 15, 25. Map p 133.*

★★ **Avenida Palace** RESTAURADORES   Opened in 1892 in grand fin-de-siècle style, this hotel has hosted well-heeled refugees from the Spanish Civil War, undercover agents during WWII, and stars of screen and stage in the '50s and '60s. A 2009 facelift restored the Belle Époque glamour, and public rooms glitter with gilt, crystal, and marble. Strategically located between Rossio square and Avenida da Liberdade, it has an English-style cocktail bar, and tea with scones is served by white-coated waiters at 5 o'clock in the palatial main salon. Up the spectacular five-story stairwell, rooms are decorated in light colors, with antique furnishings and old-master prints. *Rua 1° de Dezembro, 123. www.hotelavenida palace.pt.* ☎ *21/321-8100. 82 units. Doubles 176€–333€. Metro: Restauradores. Map p 136.*

★★★ **Casa Balthazar** CHIADO   A secret hideaway in the heart of the city, this classy bed-and-breakfast resides in a townhouse owned by the same family since 1882. The family also owns the Confeitaria Nacional, Lisbon's oldest (and arguably best) pastry shop, which guarantees a treat at breakfast time. Rooms blend modern art with antique furnishings. The best have private terraces with hot tubs and panoramic views. It's a 2-minute walk from Rossio square or the Carmo ruins. *Rua do Duque, 26. www.casabalthazarlisbon.com.* ☎ *917-085-568. 9 units. Doubles 128€–360€. Tram: 24. Map p 136*

★★ **Casa de São Mamede** PRINCIPE REAL   This solid, yellow-painted townhouse was built in

Municipal Lodging Tax

If your hotel bill is pricier than expected, chances are City Hall is to blame. In 2016, a municipal tax of 1€ per person per night was been added to the total price and your bill. Plans to double the tax to 2€ in January 2019 were underway when this book went to press. The tax applies to all guests ages 13 and older, except those traveling for medical treatment. There is a 7-night ceiling, a relief for those staying longer. The mayor says the extra revenue is needed to boost public transport, street cleaning, and other services in areas with high tourism numbers.

1758 as a magistrate's home and has been a hotel since 1948. Located on the edge of the happening Principe Real district, It's great value for the money. The good-size rooms are individually decorated in a stylishly uncluttered historical style. *Rua da Escola Politecnica, 159. www.casadesaomamede.pt.* ☎ *21/396-3166. 22 units. Doubles 90€–360€. Metro: Rato. Map p 135.*

★★★ Casa do Barão CHIADO
An aristocratic residence built after the 1755 earthquake, this bed-and-breakfast is a haven on a quiet side street in the elegant Chiado neighborhood. The spacious rooms are painted white, with soft drapes, period prints, and marble bathrooms. The top suites and rooms have private terraces and spectacular views. A courtyard pool and garden is filled with tropical vegetation. *Rua da Emenda, 84. www.casadobarao.com.* ☎ *967-944-143. 12 units. Doubles 98€–300€. Tram: 28. Map p 136.*

★★ Corpo Santo Hotel CAIS DO SODRÉ
A new addition opened in a grand 18th-century building. It's handy for the restaurants of riverside Cais do Sodré and shopping in Baixa. Staff are friendly and efficient, happy to show guests down to the basement where remains of medieval fortifications were uncovered during restoration work. The decor is inspired by Portugal's spice-trading history; rooms come complete with Nespresso machines, ultra-HD TV, and Wi-Fi sound systems. Bathrooms boast relaxing chromotherapy lighting and Molton Brown toiletries. *Largo do Corpo Santo, 25. www.corposanto hotel.com.* ☎ *21/828-8000. 79 units. Doubles 126€–408€. Metro: Cais do Sodré. Map p 136.*

★★★ Four Seasons Hotel Ritz
PARQUE   Back in the 1950s,

Lobby of the Four Seasons Ritz.

dictator António de Oliveira Salazar decided Lisbon needed a modern five-star hotel. The Ritz was the result. Still a modernist icon, it's a byword for top service and luxury overlooking Eduardo VII Park. The lounge contains one of the best collections of 20th-century Portuguese art; the **Varanda** restaurant is among the city's finest. The spa is vast, with a lap pool and lounging areas, and the bar remains the rendezvous of choice for the Lisbon elite. An extra bonus is the rooftop running track and fitness center. *Rua Rodrigo de Fonseca, 88. www.fourseasons.com/lisbon.* ☎ *21/381-1400. 282 units. Doubles 545€–850€. Metro: Marques de Pombal. Map p 135.*

★★ **Heritage Avenida Liberdade** RESTAURADORES This boutique hotel combines 18th-century grandeur with understated contemporary style thanks to Portuguese architect Miguel Câncio Martins (whose work includes Buddha Bar in Paris and the Pasha nightclub in Marrakesh). With its sumptuous sofas, low lighting, and sweet scents, the foyer is as relaxing as the spa and pool downstairs. Rooms feature stylish wallpaper, chaise longues, large, cool en-suites, and city-center views. *Avenida da Liberdade, 28. www.heritageavliberdade.pt.* ☎ *21/340-4040. 42 units. Doubles 164€–650€. Metro: Restauradores, Avenida. Map p 136.*

★ **kids HF Fénix Music** PARQUE The best of a row of mid-20th-century hotels run by the HF group just across from Eduardo VII Park. This one has a musical theme: Each room is decorated according to a style, from jazz to classical or *fado*. Live bands and DJs play music beside the rooftop pool, and high-tech sound systems turn your room into a personalized disco. The check-in desk is shaped like a drum kit, and the bar's a piano keyboard.

Groovy. *Rua Joaquim Antonio de Aguiar, 5. www.hfhotels.com.* ☎ *21/049-6570. 109 units. Doubles 77€–167€. Metro: Marques de Pombal. Map p 135.*

★★ **Hotel Britania** AVENIDA DA LIBERDADE Built in the 1940s by famed Portuguese architect Cassiano Branco, this hotel is an Art Deco gem. It has been restored to enhance its original 1940s style, with an helping of contemporary design. The location on a quiet road off the Avenida da Liberdade means you can escape the city traffic and retreat to the clubby bar, library, and lounge warmed in winter by an open fire. *Rua Rodrigues Sampaio, 17. www.heritage.pt.* ☎ *21/315-5016. 30 units. Doubles 215€–340€. Metro: Avenida. Map p 135.*

★★ **kids Hotel Convento do Salvador** ALFAMA Amid the medieval lanes of Alfama, this old convent has been converted into a hotel with Scandinavian-style minimalist rigor. There's a hip bar and a spacious patio for chilling on summer evenings. The white walls are enlivened by colorful works by contemporary Portuguese artists. If offers family and reduced-mobility rooms. It's also a hotel with a social conscience, proud of its environmental credentials and supporting children in need. *Rua do Salvador, 2B. www.conventosalvador.pt.* ☎ *21/887-2565. 43 units. Doubles 70€–157€. Tram: 28. Map p 134.*

★★ **Hotel da Estrela** ESTRELA In a quiet neighborhood featuring one of Lisbon's most beautiful gardens, this luxury boutique hotel is set in the former palace of the Counts of Paraty, a historic Brazilian town. The interiors feature quirky, colorful designs. All the spacious rooms have views over the city, River Tagus, or the hotel's own peaceful garden. For a real treat, book one of the Hästens suites kitted out by the Swedish firm reputed to make the world's most comfortable beds. There's an excellent restaurant where customers choose how much they want to pay. Many of the efficient young staff are graduates from the hotel school next door. *Rua Saraiva de Carvalho, 35. www.hoteldaestrela.com.* ☎ *21/ 190-0100. 19 units. Doubles: 99€– 157€. Metro: Rato. Map p 133.*

★★ Hotel do Chiado CHIADO

In a block restored by Pritzker Prize–winning architect Álvaro Siza Vieira after fire tore through the Chiado district in 1988, the Hotel do Chiado has a hard-to-beat location. Try to snag one of the top-floor rooms with private lawns offering views over the city and river. You can also admire the vista over cocktails on the terrace of the rooftop bar. Rooms are comfortably sized and furnished in modern-classic style with sober natural tones. It's just an elevator ride from the designer stores and centuries-old shops below. *Rua Nova do Almada, 114. www.hoteldochiado.pt.* ☎ *21/325-6100. 39 units. Doubles: 129€–569€. Metro: Baixa-Chiado. Map p 136.*

★ Hotel Duas Nações BAIXA

This old-style *pensão* has been a downtown landmark since 1875. It's recently undergone a bit of a facelift but remains a good option for travelers seeking easy-priced, no-frills accommodation in the city center. *Rua da Vitoria, 41. www. duasnacoes.com.* ☎ *21/346-0710. 54 units. Doubles 63€–180€. Metro: Baixa-Chiado. Map p 137.*

★★ International Design Hotel BAIXA

From the floor-to-ceiling windows inside the bar or the private balconies in suites and superior rooms, guests enjoy unique views over Rossio square, Lisbon's favorite meeting spot for centuries. Opened in the 1920s, it received a total makeover in 2009. The outside features creamy columns, lilac walls, and intricate wrought-iron railings. Rooms are decorated according to pop, tribal, Uurban or zen themes. The **Bastardo** restaurant is a hipster favorite. *Rua da Betesga, 3. www. idesignhotel.com.* ☎ *21/324-0990. 55 units. Doubles 135€–293€. Metro: Rossio. Map p 136.*

★ Lost Inn Lisbon Hostel

CHIADO Lisbon's hostel scene has really taken off in recent years— the city vacuums up awards on backpacker sites. This is one of the best, nestled in an 18th-century palace midway between the Bairro Alto and Cais do Sordé bar zones. Choose between budget bunks in dorms for up to 10, or a private room. There's free breakfast, a 24-hour kitchen, and a helpful team arranging activities ranging from pub crawls to surf school. *Beco dos Apostolos, 6. www.lostinnlisbon.com.* ☎ *21/347-0755. 15 units. Dorm beds from 16€. Doubles 60€–76€ Metro: Baixa-Chiado, Cais do Sodre. Map p 136.*

★ LX Boutique Hotel CAIS DO SODRÉ

Once the emblematic Hotel Braganza, a hangout of the Lisbon literary set, this hotel features prominently in José Saramago's novel *The Year of the Death of Ricardo Reis*. It was reborn in 2010 as a cool boutique hotel. Behind the sky-blue exterior, the LX maintains a historic ambience. Each floor is themed—one is dedicated to *fado* music; another evokes poet Fernando Pessoa. Decor is sober and classic with an emphasis on pastel shades and abundant natural light. The ground floor has a renowned sushi restaurant. Surrounded by the good, bad, and ugly of Lisbon's nightlife action. *Rua do Alecrim, 12. www.lxboutiquehotel. com.* ☎ *21/347-4394. 61 units.*

Doubles 90€–465€. Metro: Cais do Sodre. Map p 136.

★★ kids Martinhal Lisbon Chiado Family Suites CHIADO It calls itself the world's first elegant city-center hotel especially for families. Parents will enjoy the cool, clean design incorporated into a 19th-century mansion block. Kids will love the colorful family apartments, climbing wall, Xbox sessions, and pajama parties. The supervised kids-club activities for different age groups go from early morning till 10pm. Have lunch with the kids in the fun cafe, then head out to dinner in one of the chic Chiado restaurants nearby. *Rua das Flores, 44. www.martinhal.com/chiado. ☎ 21/002-9600. 37 units. Studios & apartments 177€–599€. Metro: Baixa-Chiado. Map p 136.*

★★★ Memmo Alfama ALFAMA Most infinity pools are blue, this one is brick-red, matching the rooftops of Alfama tumbling down the hillside below. Few places can rival the river views. The hotel is tucked away down a cul-de-sac lined with citrus trees behind the 12th-century cathedral. Modern furniture in soft creams and browns blends with ancient interior features like portions of stone wall or domed baker's ovens transformed into cozy sitting rooms. Bedrooms come with Egyptian linen sheets, LED TVs, and iStations. *Travessa Merceeiras, 27. www.memmohotels.com/alfama. ☎ 21/049-5660. 42 units. Doubles 138€–348€. Tram: 28. Map p 134.*

★★★ Memmo Principe Real PRINCIPE REAL The latest Memmo property maintains the hotel group's high standards. It blends into the hillside down a tiny lane leading out of Lisbon's trendiest neighborhood. It's got breathtaking views, elegant contemporary design (local limestone and painted tiles), and specially commissioned artworks. All rooms have Bang & Olufsen TVs and Hermes amenities; Exclusive Rooms have outdoor fireplaces. The restaurant showcases influences from the Portuguese speaking world, from Brazilian barbeque to the chocolate of São Tomé. *Rua D. Pedro V, 56. www.memmohotels.com/principereal. ☎ 21/901-6800. 41 units. Doubles 220€–509€. Tram: 24. Map p 136.*

★★★ Myriad by SANA Hotels Lisboa PARQUE DAS NAÇÕES Soaring 23 floors out of the River Tagus in the ultramodern Parque das Nações district, this landmark built in 2012 has light-filled rooms with the best sunrises in town. A bold red-and-black design runs through the rooms and public spaces, and a towering atrium comes complete with jellyfish-shaped chandeliers. The whole thing has a distinctly Dubai feel. Views get more spectacular as you rise toward the penthouse spa and fitness center. The deck of the **River Lounge** bar is the place to enjoy a waterfront port & tonic. All rooms feature a hammock seat beside the panoramic windows, where it feels like you're floating over the Tagus. *Lote 2.21.01, Parque das Nações, Rua das Cais das Naus. www.myriad.pt. ☎ 21/110-7600. 186 units. Doubles 171€–351€. Metro: Moscavide. Map p 134.*

★ My Story Tejo BAIXA The hotel reception greets guests with a funky mix of bare brick and contemporary wood and glass. This youthful hotel is just a short walk from Rossio. Rooms are simple but comfortable (although taller guests should avoid the sloping ceilings of the attic rooms). A copious breakfast is served in the barrel-arched restaurant in the modernized 19th-century building. *Rua dos Condes de Monsanto, 2. www.mystoryhotels.*

com/mystorytejo. ☎ 21/886-6182.
135 units. Doubles 77€–187€. Metro:
Rossio. Map p 137.

★★ **1908 Lisboa Hotel** INTEN-
DENTE The clue to this hotel's
vintage is right there in the name.
The restoration and reopening of
this splendid Art Nouveau construction symbolizes the regeneration of
the once-seedy Intendente neighborhood. Room decor is restrained
and comfortable. For a real treat,
book the duplex suite in the dome
that crowns the building. The
design of the cool restaurant,
Infame, plays off many of the building's original features. The location
is perfect for exploring the area's
new shops and restaurants. Largo
do Intendente Pina Manique, 6.
www.1908lisboahotel.com. ☎ 21/
880-4000. 36 units. Doubles 117€–
369€. Metro: Intendente. Map p 134.

★★★ **Olissippo Lapa Palace**
LAPA In the 1880s the Count of
Valenças made his palatial home a
high-society hub. Artists decorated
the grand salons and ballrooms; a
tropical garden was laid down with
streams and waterfalls. Since 1992,
this palace in the heart of the diplomatic quarter has been one of the
capital's most luxurious hotels,
favored by royalty, presidents, and
movie stars. Rooms are individually
decorated in keeping with the
building's heritage. A pool set amid
tranquil greenery is kept at 25°C
(77°F) from May through September, and there's a fully equipped
spa and gym. Rua Pau da Bandeira,
4. www.lapapalace.com. ☎ 21/318-
2791. 109 units. Doubles 290€–755€.
Tram: 25. Map p 133.

★★★ **Palacete Chafariz d'El
Rei** ALFAMA Seriously exotic.
Between Alfama and the river, this
over-the-top oddity was built by a
coffee tycoon in a turn-of-the-20th-
century style known as Brazilian

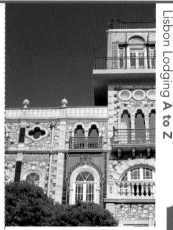

Exterior of Palacete Chafariz d'El Rei.

Nouveau. Recent restoration
respects the hotel's heritage, with
stucco ceilings, polychrome tiled
floors, and tropical plants. Rooms
are spacious, marble abounds in
the bathrooms, and there's a
charming tearoom. A true original.
Tv. do Chafariz do El-Rei, 6. www.
chafarizdelrei.com. ☎ 21/888-6150.
6 units. Doubles 342€–580€. Metro:
Terreiro do Paco. Map p 134.

★★★ **Palácio Belmonte**
CASTELO Romans built one of
the towers, and another two were
erected more than 1,000 years ago
when the Arabs ruled Lisbon. The
noble palace chambers date from
the 15th century and were home to
the family of Pedro Álvares Cabral,
discoverer of Brazil. The current
French owner invested millions to
turn the palace into an ultra-luxurious
boutique hotel. Each unique suite
is furnished with original antiques;
most have fabulous views. Inside
the lush walled garden is a black-
marble pool with a waterfall. The
palace is adorned with 18th-century
tiles, Oriental carpets underfoot,
and displays of contemporary art.
A gem. Pátio Dom Fradique, 14.

Yoga in the Terrace Suite at the Palácio Belmonte with city views.

www.palaciobelmonte.com. ☎ 21/
881-6600. 10 units. Suites 500€–
2,000€. Tram: 28. Map p 134.

★★★ Pestana Palace Hotel

ALCÂNTARA Built in 1905 by a
marquess who made a fortune in
African cocoa, this Belle Epoque
palace is the height of five-star luxury. The main building contains a
succession of ever-more-opulent
salons filled with Louis XV furniture,
gilt-framed oil paintings, crystal
chandeliers, and windows bright
with stained-glass nymphs. The palace and its surrounding gardens
are protected National Monument
sites. Most of the guest rooms are
in two modern wings overlooking
the tropical garden, but the main
palace has four grand suites.
Between Belém and downtown.
Rua Jau, 54. www.pestana.com.
☎ *21/361-5600. 190 units. Doubles
161€–305€. Tram: 15. Map p 133.*

★★★ Pousada de Lisboa

BAIXA   A flagship addition to the
renowned Pousada chain of historic
inns, this hotel occupies a strategic
location on riverside Praça do
Comércio in the heart of downtown. Once Portugal's Interior Ministry, the sturdy, pastel-painted
building today shines with art and
artifacts, the result of a 9€ million
program to restore the building's
regal features after decades of
neglect. More perks: an indoor
pool, the fine **RIB Beef & Wine** restaurant, specializing in steak, and
Castelbel toiletries in the marble
bathrooms. *Praça do Comércio,*

The pool at the Pestana Palace.

31-34. www.pousadas.pt/pt/hotel/
pousada-lisboa. ☎ 21/040-7640. 90
units. Doubles 200€–420€. Metro:
Terreiro do Paço. Map p 136.

★ **7 Hotel** BAIXA   Nothing too
fancy, just a comfortable, moder-
ately priced option in a restored
Pombaline building on a busy
downtown shopping street. Opened
in 2015, it has self-catering studios
with small kitchens as well as traditional rooms. Rua Aurea, 133.
www.7hotel.com. ☎ 21/799-6360.
37 units. Doubles 63€–256€. Metro:
Baixa-Chiado. Map p 136.

★★ **Solar dos Mouros** CASTELO
A tasteful, artsy microhotel that
opened in 2000 below the walls of
the São Jorge Castle in the oldest
part of the city. It has an intimate
atmosphere and terraces perfect
for a glass of port as you watch the
sun set over the city and river
below. Rooms feature bold color
schemes and modern art. If you
can, grab the deluxe suite with private balconies. R. do Milagre de
Santo António 6. www.solardos
mouroslisboa.com. ☎ 21/885-4940.
13 units. Doubles 119€–309€. Tram:
28. Map p 134.

★★ **Sunset Destination Hostel**
CAIS DO SODRÉ   You'd expect to
pay through the nose for accommodations with a riverside rooftop
pool. Here—if you don't mind
bunking down in a dorm—you can
do it for less than 20€. One of Lisbon's premium hostels is located
above the station where trains
depart for the coastal trip to Cascais. It has a fully equipped kitchen,
electronic lockers, a funky design
featuring French comic-strip art,
bikes to hire, and more—all in an
Art Deco gem of a building within
staggering distance of the bars on
Pink Street. It also has double rooms
with private bathrooms. Praça do
Duque de Terceira. www.sunset-
destination-hostel.lisbon-hotel.org.

☎ 21/099-7735. 14 units. Dorm
beds from 19€. Doubles 57€–119€.
Metro: Cais do Sodre. Map p 136.

★★ **The Independente** PRINCIPE
REAL   This hip hostel has bargain
bunks with some of the best views
in town. It's set in a Belle Époque
palace that was once home to Swit-
zerland's ambassador. The location
is hard to beat, on the edge of the
Bairro Alto nightlife and the chic
shopping zones of Prìncipe Real
and Chiado. In addition to mixed
and single-gender dorms for 6, 9,
or 12, it also has private rooms and
suites offering a taste of bohemian
luxury. Furniture is minimal, but the
cotton sheets are crisp and clean,
the kitchen is spacious, and a light-
filled lounge hosts movie nights
and occasional live music. Oh, a
fine restaurant/bar, the **Insólito,** is
up on the rooftop. Rua de São
Pedro de Alcantara, 81. www.the
independente.pt. ☎ 21/346-1381.
13 units. Dorm beds from 11€. Doubles 86€–271€. Tram: 24. Map p 136.

★★ **The Late Birds** BAIRRO
ALTO   Opened in 2016, this all-
male urban gay resort fits into a
modernized 18th-century building
on a quiet side street just outside
the Bairro Alto bar zone. Some
rooms have city and river views;
others overlook the secluded poor
and garden. All have a stylish, low-
key design where white predomi-
nates. The hotel hosts a tasty
Sunday brunch and regular fado
evenings. Travessa André Valente
21. www.thelatebirdslisbon.com.
☎ 93-300-0962. 12 units. Doubles
110€–180€. Tram: 28.

★★★ **Tivoli Avenida Liberdade**
AVENIDA DA LIBERDADE   Attract-
ing visiting politicians, artists, and
stars since the 1930s. The lobby
oozes old-world elegance with marble columns and velvet armchairs in
rich, deep tones. New Thai owners
gave the grand dame a facelift in

Rooftop Sky Bar at the Tivoli hotel.

2016, installing an Asian-style spa and a traditional Portuguese beer-and-shellfish restaurant. The rooftop **Sky Bar** is one of the capital's hottest spots on summer evenings. Rooms are big and airy, overlooking the tree-lined avenue or the lush garden and pool below. Portuguese movie icon Beatriz Costa liked it so much, she lived here for 30 years. *Avenida da Liberdade, 185. www.tivolihotels.com.* ☎ *21/319-8900. 285 units. Doubles 200€–375€. Metro: Avenida. Map p 135.*

★★ **Torel Palace** COLINA DE SANTANA   This charming boutique hotel occupies a pair of 1902

City views from balcony at Torel Palace.

A suite at the Valverde Hotel.

mansions in a noble, but little-visited hilltop district overlooking Av. Da Liberdade. One is painted in bold blue, the other a soft pink. The room decor reflects that mix of primary or pastel shades. Between the two buildings is a leafy garden, a patio paved with traditional tiles, and a pool that makes up for its small size with a hillside location and great views. *Rua Camara Pestana, 23. www.torelpalace.com.* ☎ *21/829-0810. 28 units. Doubles 125€–370€. Tram: 52. Map p 136.*

★★ **Travellers House** BAIXA It quickly established itself as one of Lisbon's leading hostels after opening in 2006 in an 18th-century block on super-central Rua Augusta. For bargain party vibes, grab a bunk in the dorms. Seeking privacy? Choose an en-suite double or one of four studios offering boutique-hotel charm. Staff seek to make your stay like crashing at a friend's pad—except rooms are actually clean and comfortable, the bed linens are crisp, and a free breakfast is ready and waiting for you in the morning.

Rua Augusta, 89. www.travellers house.com. ☎ *21/011-5922. 10 units. Dorm beds from 14€. Doubles 30€–48€. Metro: Baixa-Chiado. Map p 136.*

★ **Turim Terreiro do Paço Hotel** BAIXA The Turim group has a dozen comfortable, reasonably priced hotels dotted around the city. This one is perfectly placed for riverside strolls, Cais do Sodré partying, or sightseeing in the Baixa. Rooms are decorated in soft grays with some cute, colorful accessories. It's located in a typical post-1755 earthquake block. *Rua do Comercio, 9. www.turim-hotels.com.* ☎ *21/049-2590. 100 units. Doubles 84€–339€. Metro: Terreiro do Paco. Map p 137.*

★★ **Valverde Hotel** AVENIDA DA LIBERDADE There's an air of tropical elegance about this 19th-century townhouse, artistically restored in 2014. Hallmarks include lush vegetation, hardwood paneling, and retro-patterned loungers. Relax in the patio pool and enjoy modern Portuguese cooking in the

Royal Suite at the Verride Palácio Santa Catarina.

restaurant and innovative cocktails in the cozy bar. Ideal for exploring the shopping opportunities on Lisbon's chicest boulevard. *Avenida da Liberdade, 164. www.valverdehotel. com.* ☎ *21/094-0300. 25 units. Doubles 211€–446€. Metro: Avenida. Map p 135.*

★★★ Verride Palácio Santa Catarina CHIADO

Opened in 2017, this grand new addition to Lisbon's hotel scene occupies a skyline-dominating site atop one of the city's most spectacular viewpoints—a favorite spot for sunset revelers (who can get a bit noisy). Inside, marvel at the marble archways, stucco ceilings, and panels of antique blue-and-white tiles, all clustered around a monumental 18th-century staircase. On the roof, the pool and fashionable bar/ restaurant offer jaw-dropping 360-degree views. *Rua de Santa Catarina, 1. www.verridesc.pt.* ☎ *21/157-3055. 19 units. Doubles 340€–1,000€. Tram: 28. Map p 136.*

★★ York House SANTOS

To enter York House, you climb a narrow stone staircase winding between crimson walls hung with creepers and emerge into an urban garden ablaze with bougainvillea. This 17th-century convent was turned into a guest house by English ladies in 1880. It became a favorite for British travelers, including novelists Graham Greene and John le Carré. Rooms fuse original features like wooden floors and stone arches with warm, contemporary designs. The restaurant is excellent. At press time, a large construction site next door risked disturbing the tranquil charm. *Rua das Janelas Verdes, 32. www.york houselisboa.com.* ☎ *21/396-2435. 32 units. Doubles 88€–214€. Tram: 25. Map p 133.* ●

Southern Beaches

Lisbon

Montijo

A12

Rio Tejo

A2

Almada

Barreiro

A2

A33

N10

Coina

A2

A2

Paisagem
Protegida
da Arriba
Fóssil da Costa
da Caparica

A12

N10

Setúbal

ATLANTIC OCEAN

Serra da
Arrábida

N10

Lagoa de
Albufeira

③

TRÓIA PENINSULA

Sesimbra **②**

④

0 ———— 5 mi

Cabo Espichel

0 ———— 5 km

Comporta

① Costa da Caparica
② Sesimbra and
Cabo Espichel
③ Serra da Arrábida
④ Tróia and Comporta

More than any capital in Europe, Lisbon is blessed with a variety of beaches within easy reach, so it's easy to cool off even in the heat of summer. While the waters of Cascais are a familiar excursion for city-trippers, many locals prefer to head south to the Setúbal Peninsula, a sand-fringed triangle of land starting on the south bank of the Tagus, or beyond to the fashionable beaches of Tróia and Comporta. While it is possible to reach the southern beaches using a combination of bus, train, or ferry transport, a car is useful for traveling farther afield.

① ★★ **Costa da Caparica.** A 45-mile arc of fine white sand curves down the western side of Setúbal Peninsula. It changes name and character along the way but is generically known as Costa da Caparica. The northern end, closest to Lisbon, is built up and bustles in summer with families and young-sters from the suburbs on the south bank of the Tagus. It has a lively, urban feel, with restaurants grilling sardines and wandering venders selling *bolas de Berlim* (doughnuts). As you head south, crowds thin out and the beaches have a wilder feel, backed by dunes and fossil-filled cliffs. Regulars have their own beach: **Praia de São João** is popu-lar with families, **Praia do Castelo** attracts a younger crowd, kite-surfers head to blustery **Nova Vaga**, while **Praia 19** is a famed gay hangout. Areas for nudists are

Previous page: The Praia do Tamariz beach in Estoril-Cascais.

The beach at Costa da Caparica.

farther south, on the broad sands of **Fonte da Telha** and beautiful, remote **Meco**. The surf is usually good all the way down. If you prefer gentle waves, try the sand-fringed lagoon at **Lagoa de Albufeira**. Dozens of fish restaurants line the beaches, from Pé Nú, near the mouth of the Tagus, to O Bar do Peixe on Praia de Meco. *From Lisbon take TST buses 153, 155, 161 over 25 April Bridge; or the ferry to Cacilhas, then bus 124 or 135 to the beach; or the ferry to Trafaria and bus 129. A little train runs along the beach from Costa da Caparica down to Fonte da Telha.*

❷ ★★ **Sesimbra and Cabo Espichel.** Squeezed into a tight valley running to the sea, **Sesimbra** is a fishing village turned beach resort. In high season it can feel a little claustrophobic, but it has a fine sandy beach, excellent fish restaurants, and a pretty old quarter below a Moorish castle. Just out of town, unspoiled **Praia Ribeira Do Cavalo** beach looks more South Pacific than North Atlantic, with its white sand and turquoise waters. It's only reachable by a hike over the cliffs or by boat. A 30-minute drive west takes you to **Cabo Espichel**, a dramatic headland jutting over the ocean. These high, barren clifftops were sacred ground to ancient peoples, and have been a pilgrimage site since reports of an appearance by the Virgin Mary in the Middle Ages. It has a fine 16th-century convent, a lighthouse built in 1790, and a row of dinosaur footprints. Breathtaking views. *A car is advisable for exploring the coast here, but buses TST 207 and 260 reach Sesimbra from Lisbon's Praça de Espanha in about an hour. Buses 201 and 205 run from Sesimbra to Cabo Espichel.*

❸ ★★★ **Serra da Arrábida.** This high-range, 40-minute drive south of Lisbon is a marvel of nature. The slopes are covered in Mediterranean scrubland rolling down to the coast, where a succession of crescent beaches offer golden sand and calm blue waters. **Portinho da Arrábida** is the biggest and best-known. The views across the Sado estuary to the sandbars of Tróia are amazing. Adding to the natural beauty is a 16th-century convent with white walls and red-tile roofs clinging to the hillside; visits by appointment only (☎ **21/219-7620**). Although the hills are now a protected natural park, they were scarred by a cement factory built in 1904 and still functioning. It's a shock when you drive past, but not noticeable on the beaches or up in the hills. The nearby town of **Setúbal** is one of Portugal's busiest ports. It has a pretty downtown, a fabulous fish market, and restaurants specializing in deep-fried cuttlefish. *Regular trains run from Lisbon's Roma-Areeiro station to Setúbal. Take TST Lisbon-to-Setúbal buses 561, 562,*

Swimmers at Comporta Beach.

563, 565, 583. In the summer shuttle buses run from Setúbal to the Arrábida beaches, where there is limited access for cars.

❹ ★★★ **Tróia & Comporta.** The Tróia peninsula is a 10-mile sliver of sand dividing the Atlantic from the Sado River estuary (a popular spot for dolphins). Around its tip and down the ocean side is an unbroken stretch of fine sand backed by pine forest. A small resort has hotels, a casino, and a marina at the northernmost point. To the south, beaches are seemingly unending. Here lies the village of **Comporta,** a favorite hideaway of Lisbon's fashionable set (and international celebrities like Madonna and Philippe Starck). The village boasts bobo boutiques and avocado brunches, but the pristine beach is the big attraction. The sand curves in a great arc for

A beach along the Serra da Arrábida.

Where to Stay & Dine

Lodging: **Pousada Castelo de Palmela** occupies a historic hilltop castle overlooking Setúbal (www.pousadas.pt; ☎ **21/235-1226;** doubles 110€–175€). **Tróia Design Hotel** is a glitzy modern tower on the waterfront (www.troiadesignhotel.com; ☎ **26/549-8000;** doubles 104€–161€). **Sana Sesimbra** offers nautical style right on the beach (www.sanahotels.com; ☎ **21/228-9000;** doubles 68€–280€). Dining: **Ribamar** (www.marisqueiraribamar.com mains 18€–22€) serves seafood right on the Sesimbra seafront. **Santiago** (☎ **26/522-1688;** mains 7€–13€) is Setúbal's king of fried cuttlefish. **Porto Santana** (☎ **26-562-2517;** mains 9€–14€) prepares traditional dishes in historic Alcácer do Sal, inland from Comporta.

miles—to the north you can see the Arrábida hills; to the south the strand just goes on and on. Development is sparse, but expect a few excellent beach restaurants and bars. Comporta has one irritation:

mosquitoes, which breed in nearby rice paddies and can be a real hassle in the evenings. *Foot and car ferries run from Setúbal to Tróia. To go beyond to Comporta, you really need a car.*

Comporta Beach.

Cascais & Estoril

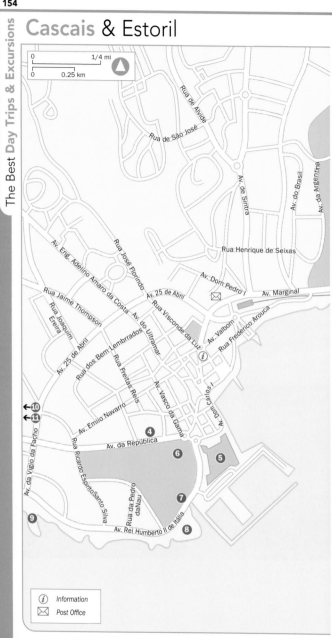

Rua de Alvide
Rua de São José
Av. de Sintra
Av. do Brasil
Av. da Argentina
Rua Henrique de Seixas
Av. Eng. Adelino Amaro da Costa
Rua José Florindo
Av. Dom Pedro I
Av. Marginal
Av. 25 de Abril
Rua Visconde da Luz
Rua Jaime Thompson
Rua Joaquim Ereira
Av. do Ultramar
Rua Frederico Arouca
Rua dos Bem Lembrrados
Av. 25 de Abril
Rua Freitas Reis
Av. Valbom
Av. Vasco da Gama
Av. Dom Carlos I
Av. Emílio Navarro
Av. da República
Av. da Vigia do Facho
Rua Ricardo EspíritoSanto Silva
Rua da Pedro daNau
Av. Rei Humberto II de Itália

4
6
5
7
8
9
10
11

| | Information |
| | Post Office |

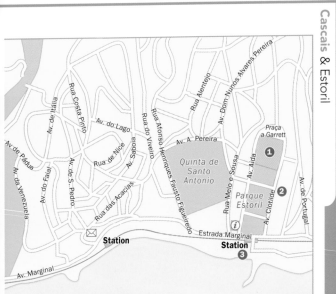

1. Estoril Casino
2. Palácio Estoril Hotel
3. Praia de Tamariz
4. Casa das Histórias Paula Rego
5. Citadela
6. Parque Marechal Carmona
7. Museu Conde de Castro Guimarães
8. Casa Santa Marta
9. Boca do Inferno
10. Praia do Guincho
11. Cabo da Roca

This pair of stony seaside resorts are just a short ride along a scenic waterside train line. They offer the easiest way out of the city and onto sandy beaches, elegant avenues and gardens, and some serious mansions. Follow the coast beyond Cascais for some nature in the raw, where a rocky shore leads to fabulous Guincho beach and the mountains along Europe's most westerly point.

Estoril's Praia do Tamariz.

❶ ★★ Estoril. Best known for Europe's biggest casino (p 117), Estoril also has a string of sandy beaches. The biggest and best-known is **Praia de Tamariz,** a couple of steps from the railway station. It's overseen by restaurants, pool clubs, and some of the patrician abodes built when Estoril first took off as a Belle Époque bathing resort. Leading from the sea, the casino gardens are filled with lofty palms and backed by buildings from the 1930s—the grandest of which is the luxurious **Palácio Estoril Hotel**. During WWII, it filled with wealthy refugees (including much of Europe's deposed royalty) and became a nest of spies. Writers Graham Green and Ian Fleming were both here with British intelligence. Estoril's mix of sunshine and celebrity led to its fame as the "Portuguese Riviera." The golf and tennis clubs are among the country's best. **Pastelaria Garrett,** opened in 1934, is a famed cafe/pastry shop. *Estoril station is a 36-minute train ride from Lisbon's Cais do Sodré.*

❷ ★★ Downtown Cascais. Take the train to the end of the line a few minutes beyond Estoril. Alternatively, you can walk into Cascais along the seafront promenade. Central Cascais maintains a core of cobbled streets packed with little shops and pavement cafes. Three **sandy beaches** lie in the heart of the city, which also has a large park,

Surfing in Cascais.

Parque Marechal Carmona. Once a small fishing port, Cascais became known as the "royal village" when the Portuguese monarchs set up home here. Later came exiled royal families from Italy, Spain, Romania, and Bulgaria. Britain's former King Edward VIII and Wallis Simpson, the woman he

gave up the throne for, also set up home here for a while. Portugal's presidents still stay in the former royal summer house in the imposing **Citadela,** which guards the harbor; it includes a luxury hotel, shops, and art galleries. Past the citadel are a couple of interesting museums. The **Museu Conde de Castro Guimarães,** housed in a mock-Gothic mansion, is packed with an aristocratic collection that includes Indo-Portuguese furniture and books from the 1500s. On a photogenic cove almost next door is **Casa Santa Marta,** an emblematic early 20th-century home, and a blue-and-white-striped beacon that hosts the **Lighthouse Museum.**

③ ★★ Casa das Histórias Paula Rego. Cascais' best museum is dedicated to Portugal's greatest living artist. Born in 1935, Paula spent much of her childhood around Cascais and maintains close ties to the city even though she lived much of her life in London.

The twin red pyramids of the Casa das Histórias Paula Rego museum.

Where to Stay & Dine

Lodging: **Farol Hotel** is a stylish 19th-century mansion located right on the Cascais coastline, with designer rooms and dreamy ocean views (www.farol.com.pt; ☎ 21/482-3490; doubles 124€–382€). In the same family for generations, **Casa da Pérgola** is a charming turn-of-the-century house in the heart of Cascais with a glorious garden (www.pergolahouse.pt; ☎ 21/484-0040; doubles 64€–188€). **Forteleza do Guincho,** a luxury 17th-century cliff fort overlooking the surf crashing on to Guincho beach, boasts a Michelin-starred restaurant (www.fortalezadoguincho.com; ☎ 21/487-0491; doubles 120€–380€).

Dining: **Cimas** (www.cimas.com.pt; mains 18€–32€) opened as an Estoril English bar during WWII. It serves refined food amid mock-Elizabethan decor with an emphasis on game. **Eduardo das Conquilhas** (www.eduardodasconquilhas.com; ☎ 21/457-3303; mains 7.50€–20€) has been serving up superlative seafood for 50 years in Parede, a couple of stations before Estoril. Tuck into treats like lobster and shellfish rice at **O Faroleiro** (www.faroleiro.com; ☎ 26/487-0225; mains 19€–60€), accompanied by panoramic views of Guincho and the mountains.

The museum opened in 2009 and gives an overview of her work, from early abstractions to the dark, disturbing portraits of powerful female characters for which she has become best-known. The striking

Cycling along Praia do Guincho.

Boca do Inferno (the Mouth of Hell), an ancient rock cavern whipped by the sea. A plaque tells of occultist Aleister Crowley, who faked his own death here in 1930, only to show up 3 weeks later at a Berlin art exhibition. From here you can hike 5 miles, hire a bike, or catch a bus (405, 415) to Guincho. You'll pass a surf-battered rocky coastline, lighthouses, fortresses, and fish restaurants along the way. The trip is worth it: **Praia do Guincho** is a stunning half-mile beach, broad and sandy. It's overlooked by the Sintra mountains and **Cabo da Roca** (p 39), the western edge of Europe. It's blustery here, better for wind- and kite-surfing than lying in the sun.

Exploring the seaside cliffs of Cabo da Roca.

building with its twin red pyramids was designed by Pritzker Prize–winning architect Eduardo Souto de Moura. *Avenida da República, 300. www.casadashistoriaspaularego. com.* ☎ *21-482-6970. Admission 5€ adults; 2.50€ seniors and students; free for children 12 and under. Tues–Sun 10am–5:30pm.*

❹ ★★★ **The coast to Guincho.** Head out of Cascais along the coast, with the Atlantic on your left and a row of millionaires' mansions on your right. Pause to take a look at the **Grande Real Villa Itália**, once the home of King Umberto II of Italy, now a luxurious hotel. A bracing 10-minute walk leads to

Casa da Pergola.

Sintra, Mafra & Ericeira

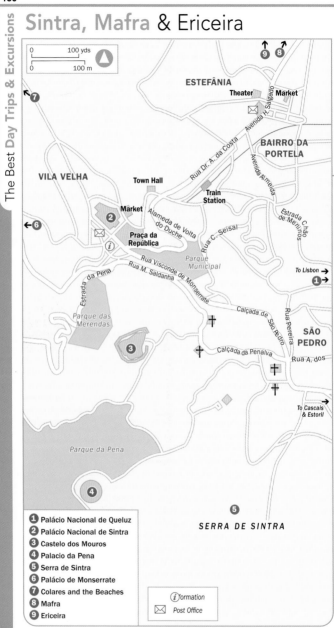

ESTEFÂNIA

Theater   Market

BAIRRO DA PORTELA

VILA VELHA

Town Hall

Market

Train Station

Rua Dr. A. da Costa

Avenida H. Salgado

Avenida Almeida

Estrada Chão de Meninos

Alameda de Volta do Duche

Praça da República

Rua C. Seisal

Rua Visconde de Monserrate

Rua M. Saldanha

Parque Municipal

Estrada da Pena

Parque das Merendas

Calçada de São Pedro

Rua Pereira

SÃO PEDRO

Calçada da Penalva

Rua A. dos

Parque da Pena

SERRA DE SINTRA

To Lisbon →
1 →

To Cascais & Estoril →

0   100 yds
0   100 m

1 Palácio Nacional de Queluz
2 Palácio Nacional de Sintra
3 Castelo dos Mouros
4 Palacio da Pena
5 Serra de Sintra
6 Palácio de Monserrate
7 Colares and the Beaches
8 Mafra
9 Ericeira

*i*formation
✉ Post Office

If you can do only one trip out of Lisbon, make it Sintra. Just a short train ride away, this fairy-tale location of lush, forested hills was called a "glorious Eden" by Lord Byron. Among the vegetation, Arab warriors built a hilltop castle, hermits lived in troglodyte convents and, for centuries, the royal family, Portuguese aristocracy, and foreign magnates erected fantastic palaces. As if that weren't enough, this romantic UNESCO World Heritage site (p 37) produces excellent wine and has a wild and wonderful coastline with some great hidden beaches. The ride to Sintra from Rossio station in the heart of downtown Lisbon takes 40 minutes. Just north of Sintra, the massive convent and palace complex of Mafra and the surf center at Ericeira are also well worth a visit.

Gardens of the 18th-century Queluz National Palace.

❶ ★★ Palácio Nacional de Queluz.

You'll come across this splendid rococo palace before you even get to Sintra. Portugal's "mini-Versailles" was built in the 1740s as a summer residence for Queen Maria I and her consort King Pedro. In her later years the queen was hidden away in this suburban retreat to hide her madness from the people of Lisbon. Its exterior is a pastel fantasy in blue, yellow, and ochre with white trim like icing on a wedding cake, and the gardens are majestic. Emperor Pedro I, who led Brazil to independence in 1822, was born and died here. Later leaders to drop by for a night or two included U.S. Presidents Eisenhower, Carter, and Reagan, as well as Prince Charles and Diana, Princess of Wales. The sumptuous interiors are certainly fit for a princess, a riot of crystal, tropical frescos, gilt appliqués, mirrored walls, Flemish tapestries, and Chinese porcelain. A fine hotel, the **Pousada Palácio de Queluz,** is located in an 18th-century annex, and across the street, the renowned restaurant **Cozinha Velha** is in the old palace kitchens. *Largo Palácio de Queluz.*

Sintra National Palace.

www.parquesdesintra.pt. ☎ 21/434-3860. Admission 10€ adults; 8.50€ seniors and ages 8–17; free for children 8 and under. Apr–Oct daily 9am–6pm; Nov–Mar daily 9am–5pm. Train: Queluz-Belas. Bus: 101.

② ★★★ **Palácio Nacional de Sintra.** The pair of outsized chimneys towering over this white-painted palace are what first grabs your attention when you arrive in downtown Sintra. Known locally as the Palácio da Vila (Town Palace), in contrast with the other royal abodes up on the hilltop (see below), this delightfully eclectic pile traces its roots back to the days of Arab rule, starting in the 8th ventury when the emirs of Lisbon had a residence here. Portugal's first king, Afonso Henriques, moved in after he conquered Lisbon in 1147. Today's building is a mishmash of styles from Moorish to Manueline, Gothic to Renaissance. Highlights include the **Sala das Pegas** (Magpie Room). Its multitude of black-and-white birds were painted on the ceiling on the order of King João I (1385–1483)

to represent the gossipy ladies at court after his English wife Philippa of Lancaster found him kissing one of them. Other salons have painted ceilings decorated with swans or mermaids. One of the grandest, the **Sala dos Brasões** is crowned with a dome bearing the coats of arms of 72 noble families. The whole thing makes a fascinating tour through history, from the kitchens beneath those conical chimneys to courtyards filled with arabesque *azulejos* and the room were King Afonso VI died after being deposed and imprisoned by his brother in 1683. *Largo Rainha Dona Amélia. www.parquesdesintra.pt.* ☎ *21-910-6840. Admission 10€ adults; 8.50€ seniors and ages 8–17; free for children 8 and under. Apr–Oct daily 9:30am–6:30pm; Nov–Mar daily 9:30am–5:30pm.*

③ ★★ **Castelo dos Mouros.** Vertigo sufferers should think twice about climbing up to the Castle of the Moors. It was built in the 8th and 9th-centuries by Arab warriors as a mountaintop fortress and lookout post for surveying the countryside and coastline for miles around. Iron Age remains suggest that it was also the site of an earlier fort. Despite imposing double walls, the castle was sacked by Norwegian raiders in 1109, and 4 decades later was handed over to King Afonso Henriques without a fight after the fall of Lisbon. These days, the battlements form a romantic ruin, the best place for views over the city of Sintra in the valley below, Pena Palace on the opposite peak, and the blue Atlantic Ocean in the distance. You can visit archaeological sites to see remains of a Muslim village and a medieval Christian burial ground. Walking the ramparts can be tiring on the feet, especially if you hike up to the **Royal Tower**, but you can recover in the modern cafe and visitor center. *Estrada da Pena. www. parquesdesintra.pt.* ☎ *21/923-7300. Admission 8€ adults; 6.50€ seniors*

and ages 6–17; free for children 5 and under. Apr–Oct daily 9:30am–7pm; Nov–Mar daily 10am–5pm. It you don't want to hike a mile up through the forest, the 434 bus makes a circular route from the station and central Sintra every 15 min.

④ ★★★ **Palacio da Pena.** This fairy-tale mountaintop castle is Sintra's most recognizable building. Its eccentric outline of domes and towers can be seen for miles around. Up close it's even odder, with crenelated turrets, Moorish domes, conical towers, Manueline arches, and doorways guarded by diabolical statues. Everything comes in a candy-colored array of shades, from shocking pink to taxicab yellow. It's often been compared to Bavaria's fanciful Neuschwanstein (which inspired Disney) but actually predates the German castle by 30 years. The similarities are not coincidental, however; both were built by German monarchs inspired by 19th-century ideas of the romantic Middle Ages. Pena was the labor of love of Prince Ferdinand of Saxe-Coburg and Gotha-Koháry, who became prince consort of Portugal in 1837 after his marriage to Queen Maria II. Ferdinand was fascinated by the verdant hills of Sintra and their medieval remains, so he combined elements of just about every architectural era to create this extraordinary pastiche. The interior shows how the royals lived in the final years of the monarchy, packed with period furnishings and portraits. There are poignant works by King Carlos I, a talented painter who was gunned down by republican revolutionaries in 1908. The palace perches on a rocky outcrop surrounded by magnificent gardens that range from formal French-style

Pena National Palace in Sintra.

lawns and flowerbeds to thick forests filled with exotic flora brought here from around the world. *Estrada da Pena. www.parquedesintra.pt. ☎ 21/910-5340. Admission 14€ adults; 12.50€ seniors and ages 6–17; free for children 5 and under. Daily: Apr–Oct 9:45am–6:15pm; Nov–Mar 10am–5pm. It you don't want to hike the steep mile up through the forest, the 434 bus makes a circular route from the station and central Sintra every 15 min.*

⑤ ★★★ **Serra De Sintra.** Almost all of the Sintra mountains down to the Atlantic coast form a protected natural park covering 56 square miles. You can explore this unique landscape over miles of winding lanes, hiking tracks, and mountain-bike and horse-riding

trails. It's bursting with some 900 species of native and exotic plants that thrive in Sintra's relatively cool, damp microclimate. If you're lucky, you'll spot peregrine falcon or Bonelli's eagles soaring overhead. Between October and April, the gardens and parks bloom with camellias, with the most famed collection in Pena park. In addition to natural wonders, the serra is dotted with manmade treasures. Deep in the forest, the Convento dos Capuchos has a lost-world feel. Franciscan monks carved their convent into the rocks and lived an isolated troglodyte existence in moss-covered, cork-lined cells. King Felipe II of Spain, then the most powerful man in Europe, visited in 1581 and declared it one of two places he

Eating & Staying in Sintra

Lodging: A fabulous luxury retreat set amid the forest and lakes of the Sintra hills, **Penha Longa Resort** boasts world-class golf, a spa voted best in Portugal, and several restaurants including the Michelin-starred **LAB** and **Midori,** serving amazingly creative Japanese cuisine (Estrada da Lagoa Azul; www.penhalonga.com; ☎ 21/924-9011; doubles 111€–445€). The oldest hotel on the Iberian Peninsula, **Lawrence's** is a charming boutique option in Sintra town, with an excellent restaurant. Bryon wrote here, and it features in the classic Portuguese novel *The Maias* (Rua Consigliéri Pedroso, 38-40; www.lawrenceshotel.com; ☎ 21/910-5500; doubles 180€–240€). **Casa Paço D'Ilhas** is a laidback surfer hangout in a beautifully restored country cottage close to Ericeira's best waves (Estrada da Junceira; www.casapacodilhas.com; ☎ 96/005-5361; doubles 50€–155€; minimum 7-night stay July–Aug).
Dining: For remarkable seafood and architecture, head to **Azenhas do Mar** (www.azenhasdomar.com; ☎ 21/928-0739; mains 18€–32€), cut into a cliff face in a village of the same name. **Adega do Saraiva** (Largo do Paquete, Nafarros; ☎ 21/929-0106; mains 9.50€–17.50€) is a big, bustling country restaurant renowned for its roast meat. **Café Saudade** (Av. Miguel Bombarda 6; ☎ 21/242-8804; mains 5.50€–7.95€) is a charming cafe for light meals and Sintra's delicious *queijadas* (cinnamon mini-cheesecakes).

loved most in his realm (the Escorial Monastery outside Madrid was the other). In a valley below Palacio da Pena is an Alpine chalet with a romantic story. After the death of Queen Maria II, her husband King Ferdinand fell in love with an American opera singer Elise Friedericke Hensler (1836–1929) and, defying social convention, married her. The couple lived quietly in the Chalet da Condessa d'Edla, entertaining artists and cultivating their gardens. The restored chalet and gardens are open to the public. Another surprising spot in the hills is the Santuario da Peninha, a pilgrimage spot since the Middle Ages, with soaring views over the Atlantic. Families of seafarers would come to pray to the Virgin Mary for the safety of loved ones at sea. *www.parquesdesintra.pt. The 434 bus will drop you at the chalet. You'll need a car or sturdy hiking boots to reach the more remote parts of the serra.*

⑥ ★★ Palácio de Monserrate. "A scene from 1001 Nights, a fairytale vision," was how Hans Christian Andersen described this Moorish fantasy clinging to a Sintra hillside. Like Quinta da Regaleira (p 37) and Seteais Palace (p 37), this is one of Sintra's great privately built palaces, raised by English merchant Francis Cook in the 1860s. Like others at the time, he was inspired by romantic notions of Portugal's Islamic past, building an Oriental-style villa with an interior that recalls Granada's Alhambra. Not that he wasn't open to other influences: the central red dome takes the Duomo in Florence as its model. Lovingly restored in the early 2000s, the palace is surrounded by **landscaped parkland** filled with statues, grottoes, ornamental ponds, and exotic vegetation including giant ferns from New

Zealand and a plantation of Mexican agave. *Rua Barbosa do Bocage. www.parquesdesintra.pt. ☎ 21/923-7300. Admission 8€ adults; 6.50€ seniors and ages 6–17; free for children 5 and under. Apr–Oct daily 9:30am–6:15pm; Nov–Mar daily 10am–5pm. Bus 435 from Sintra.*

⑦ ★★ Colares and the beaches. The best way to reach the coast from Sintra is to take the **Tram**. Rickety open carriages trundle down the hillside hourly in the summer, a 40-minute trip to reach the broad sandy beach and seafood restaurants at **Praia das Maçãs**. It stops along the way at **Colares,** a pretty village that produces excellent wines (several wineries are open to visitors). If you have a car, you can explore the coast to Europe's **most westerly point at windswept Cabo da Roca** (p 39), marvel at the cliff-clinging village of **Azenhas do Mar,** or swim off unspoiled beaches like **Praia da Ursa** or **Praia da Adraga** (which has another excellent fish restaurant).

⑧ ★★★ Palácio de Mafra. A Brazilian gold rush made King João V (1707–1750) one of Europe's richest monarchs. He pumped money into building projects, none grander than this vast palace, church, and convent complex. Sparing no expense, João engaged artists and artisans from around Europe. The 92 church bells were founded in Antwerp, marble was shipped from Carrera, paintings and sculptures ordered from Rome. German architect Johann Friedrich Ludwig was charged with building one of the largest royal residences on the continent. At the center rises a baroque **basilica** with a white limestone facade flanked by

The Best Day Trips & Excursions

Ericeira.

twin towers and capped by a 200-foot cupola. The palace stretches out over 100 yards on either side. In all, it covers an area of five-and-a-half football fields. Construction took 13 years and mobilized 45,000 workers (some 1,350 were killed). Author José Saramago captures the times in his novel *Baltasar and Blimunda*. Tours take in the huge barrel-roofed church, an austere monks' hospital, and sumptuous royal apartments, but the standout is João's great library containing more than 36,000 leather-bound books. *Terreiro D. João V, Mafra. www.palaciomafra.gov.pt.* ☎ *26/181-7550. Admission 6€ adults; 3€ seniors and students; free for children 12 and under. Wed–Mon 9:30am–4:45pm. Mafrense buses make the 20-mile run to the palace from Lisbon's Campo Grande station and from Sintra.*

9 ★★ **Ericeira**. This pretty little fishing port north from Sintra is one of Portugal's prime surf locations. Beaches like **Praia Ribeira d'Ilhas** and **Praia do Norte** draw wave riders from around the world. On summer evenings, the bars and pavement cafes fill and the white-washed clifftop town buzzes. Food lovers come for the famed seafood in waterfront restaurants like **Furnas** and **Golfinho Azul**. Ericeira also has history: Portugal's last king Manuel II was staying in nearby Mafra when the republican revolution broke out in 1910. He fled from the little port to exile in England, never to return. During WWII, its hotels were home to refugees from around Europe fleeing Nazi persecution. *Mafrense buses run to Ericeira from Lisbon's Campo Grande station and from Sintra.* ●

The Savvy Traveler

Before You Go

Portuguese Tourism Office
In the US: 866 Second Ave., 8th Floor, New York, NY 10017 (☎ 646-723-0220). **In Canada:** 438 University Ave., Suite 1400, Toronto, Ontario M4W 3B8 (☎ 416-921-4925). **In the UK:** 11 Belgrave Sq., London SW1X 8PP (☎ 0845-355-1212).

The Best Time to Go

Lisbon is a year-round destination, a firm favorite with European city-trip travelers and increasingly with travelers from farther afield. But the summer months of **July and August** are still the busiest, when the city is packed with tourists while many *Lisboetas* leave on vacation. High summer usually guarantees good weather for anybody hoping to combine a stay in the capital with some down time on Portugal's famed beaches. **June** is party month in Lisbon, when the city celebrates its patron Saint Anthony with open-air concerts and street parties on warm evenings. It's great for lively atmosphere, less so if you're seeking peace and quiet. **Winter** months are quieter, the weather is usually mild, and theaters and museums host a full slate of events. It's a good time for off-season hotel deals. Many visitors favor **April** and **May,** when the weather warms, markets fill with strawberries and sweet juicy loquats, and wildflowers coat the surrounding hillsides. **September** and **October** see the city still warm and fizzing with energy after the summer break.

Festivals & Special Events

For full info and updates on festivals, see **www.visitlisboa.com.** You can buy tickets for events and check what's on at **www.ticketline.pt** or **www.bol.pt.**

SPRING. Foodies flock to the annual **Peixe em Lisboa** (www.peixemlisboa.com) gastronomic festival for 10 days in April, featuring cooking by world-renowned chefs, workshops, gourmet markets, and judging of the world's best *pastel de nata* (custard tarts). The **IndieLisboa** (www.indielisboa.com) showcases independent cinema from around the world at venues across the city. May draws tennis fans to the **Millennium Estoril Open (**www.millenniumestorilopen.com) Portugal's only event on the ATP tour. Tickets are hot property so book early.

SUMMER. In June, Lisbon goes wild for the **Festa de Santo António** in honor of the city's patron saint, whose festival day is June 13. Events include a mass wedding of couples from parishes around Lisbon in the Sé cathedral. Later in the evening, the **Marchas Populares** take place down Avenida da Liberdade where the city's neighborhoods compete to produce the best traditional costumes, song, and dance, cheered on by huge crowds. When it's over, winners and losers head back to their districts for a long night of street partying. The carousing actually gets underway weeks before the big day with regular nights of singing, dancing, and drinking in alleys hung with bunting and colored lights. June is also start of the **sardine season,** with makeshift barbecues set up on the streets to grill shoals of the little fish. It's estimated the Portuguese eat 35 million sardines in June, washed down with gallons of red wine and chilled beer.

Besides the street parties, City Hall organizes a program of open-air concerts with music ranging

Useful Websites

www.visitportugal.com: The excellent official website of Turismo de Portugal, the country's national tourist board, is packed with tips and practical information on traveling to the capital and beyond.

www.visitlisboa.com: Official tourism website of Turismo de Lisboa Visitors & Convention Bureau.

www.lisbonlux.com: Beautiful photos and insider tips produced by locals in English and Portuguese.

www.timeout.com/lisbon: The international guide's Lisbon edition has fast-moving listings of what's happening in town.

www.atlaslisboa.com: The self-proclaimed "people's guide" to Lisbon offers insider tips ranging from dealing with drug dealers to finding rock-climbing sites.

www.sintraromantica.net: Packed full of ideas for visitors to the romantic hillside town of Sintra.

www.visitcascais.com: Official information on the beach suburbs of Cascais and Estoril.

from jazz and *fado* to symphony orchestras (www.culturanarua.pt). Lisbon has also become a major venue for big summer music festivals. Among the most star-studded are **Nos Alive** (www.nosalive.com) and **Super Bock Super Rock** (www.superbocksuperrock.pt), held at riverside venues at opposite ends of the city in July, and **Rock in Rio** (www.rockinriolisboa.sapo.pt), which takes place every 2 years. Big names at recent shows have included the Killers, Bruce Springsteen, Katy Perry, Muse, and Bruno Mars.

Jazz aficionados can chill at the **EDP Cool Jazz** festival (www.edpcooljazz.pt), held along the coast in Cascais in July, or at **Jazz em Agosto** (www.gulbenkian.pt/jazzemagosto) in the leafy gardens of the Gulbenkian Museum the following month. Soccer fans can see storied Lisbon rivals Benfica and Sporting in action during the **Primeira Liga** (www.ligaportugal.pt) season from August through May.

FALL. The genre's top stars perform Lisbon's traditional *fado* music in late September during the **Santa Casa Alfama** (www.santacasaalfama.com) festival at iconic locations across the medieval Alfama neighborhood. An eclectic mix of musicians from Portugal and around the world perform at **Misty Fest** (www.mistyfest.com) in October and November, while admirers of classical music can look forward to the opening of the opera season at the 18th-century **Teatro Nacional de São Carlos** (www.tnsc.pt).

In October, the Portuguese fashion industry's main event, **Moda Lisboa** (www.modalisboa.com), attracts designers and models from around the world, and the **LEFFEST (Lisbon and Sintra Film Festival)** (www.leffest.com/en) always draws a scattering of top names from Hollywood and world cinema.

WINTER. In the weeks running up to **Christmas**, shoppers pour into Lisbon to admire the decorative lights that festoon the Baixa district and line the Avenida da Liberdade. It's also the time to indulge in festive treats like the fruit-bedecked *bolo rei* cake or *rabanadas* (French toast soaked in port and cinnamon).

Lisbon's **New Year's Eve** revolves around a mega party in the riverside Praça do Comércio with local bands and fireworks at midnight over the waters of the Tagus. Festivities continue into the wee small hours in the city's bars and clubs. Stay-at-homes traditionally welcome in the new year by banging pots and pans from their windows.

The Lisbon **Carnaval** in February does not match the glamour of Rio or Venice, but plenty of Carnaval parties rage late into the night.

The Weather

Lisbon's has arguably the best climate of any European capital. The city gets 2,799 hours of sunshine a year, more than any capital on mainland Europe (La Valetta, on the island of Malta, beats Lisbon by a nose). Although average highs reach the low 80s°C in the hottest months of July and August, there's usually a cooling breeze off the Atlantic to ensure that things don't overheat. Winters are gentle, with average highs of around 60°C in January and December. Many people like the mild spring and fall best. Rainy days are rare, but when they come, the downpour can be torrential and street traders do a roaring trade in umbrellas for travelers caught in the drenching. Be warned, though: The weather may be balmy, but the water off Lisbon's beaches is notoriously chilly, rarely sneaking over the mid 60s°C even at the height of summer.

Cellphones

Most modern North American cellphones work in Europe, but roaming charges can be high. Check with your provider to make sure yours will work and if you can activate an international service to cut costs. If you plan on making regular calls in Portugal, it can be cheaper to buy a local phone or a Portuguese SIM card. The process is relatively hassle-free and offered by the three main telecom companies: Vodafone (www.vodafone.pt), MEO (www.meo.pt) and NOS (www.nos.pt), each of which has shops around Lisbon. Vodafone has an easy-to-understand English language section on its website that explains what you need to do and how much it costs. A prepaid, rechargeable SIM card with 500 minutes/text messages to Portuguese and European numbers, and 5 gigabytes of data costs 20€. Wi-Fi is widely available in hotels, cafes, and other public places.

Car Rentals

With narrow streets and limited parking, Lisbon's historic core makes driving a challenge. As an alternative, **taxis** are cheap, **subway, streetcar, and bus service** is effective, and **walking** is a pleasure in the compact city center. The beach resorts along the coast to Cascais and the historic hill town of Sintra are easily reachable by **train.**

If, however, you want to explore less-accessible day-trip destinations like the idyllic beaches of Comporta or the dramatic coast beyond Sintra, having your own car is certainly useful. Rental companies at Lisbon Airport include **Avis-Budget** (☎ 21/843-5550), **Europcar** (☎ 21/840-1176), **Hertz** (☎ 21/942-6300), **Sixt** (☎ 21/847-0661) **Goldcar** (☎ 21/841-3768), and **Guerin** (☎ 21/841-3768).

Getting There

By Plane
Humberto Delgado International Airport (www.airport-lis.com) is Portugal's main gateway to the world. It's conveniently close to the city center, giving visitors a dramatic first look at Lisbon as their plane approaches the runway. The airport is modern and well-stocked with shops and cafes, but the growing increase in traffic sometimes means longer lines at passport control and longer wait times at luggage carousals during peak hours.

Taxi lines outside Arrivals can also be challenging. To avoid them, insiders head to Departures and grab a cab dropping off there. **Taxi** fares to downtown average around 12€. The car park in front of Departures is also the place to pick up cars from Uber and other ride-hailing services.

Aerobus (www.aerobus.pt) is an efficient shuttle bus service running on two lines from the airport into the city. Line 1 operates on a circular route to the downtown with 18 stops close to main landmarks and hotels; buses run every 20 minutes from 7am to 11pm. Line 2 heads to the business district around the Sete Rios bus and train station. Tickets cost 4€ from the stand outside Arrivals, or 3.60€ online. Tickets are valid 24 hours and can be used to travel around the city on the Aerobus routes.

There's a **subway** station at the airport, but you'll need to change lines to reach the most popular downtown destinations.

By Car
Portugal has one of Europe's most extensive **toll-highway networks** linking Lisbon to all of Portugal and though Spain to the rest of Europe. It takes less than 6 hours to cover the 390 miles from the Spanish capital of **Madrid,** with some interesting potential stopovers like the Spanish city of Mérida with its spectacular Roman remains, or the medieval Portuguese towns of Évora and Elvas. Drivers from London or Paris take the **E-80 highway,** which runs through northern Spain, skirting historic locations such as San Sebastian, Burgos, and Salamanca. Spain and Portugal are both in the European Union's free-movement zone, meaning no frontier controls on the highways.

Portugal's fast *autostrada* highways are mostly run on a **toll system.** If hiring a car in Portugal, check to see if it is equipped with a device that allows you to use the "Via Verde" system, passing through fast lanes at toll gates while the toll is automatically added to your rental bill. *Note:* If crossing into Portugal in a foreign-registered car, you may need to stop at a Welcome Point close to some frontier crossings to purchase a pass for a new electronic toll system introduced on certain roads. Alternatively, you can buy a prepaid toll card online (www.tollcard.pt.)

By Train
Portugal is not yet connected to Europe's high-speed train network, and international rail connections are limited. From **Madrid,** the 10-hour overnight train to Lisbon costs 61€ to 185€, depending on whether you get a regular seat or a luxury sleeping berth. Coming from **Paris** you'll ride the French high-speed train network to Irun/Hendaye on the France-Spain border and connect with the **Sud Expresso** sleeper train that runs nightly to Lisbon; the journey takes around 12 hours. There's a dining car and

first-class private cabins with showers for two; cheaper berths are available in four-person cabins. One-way prices range from 70€ for a seat to 201€ for a "grand class" single cabin complete with private bathroom. Tickets can be booked online from the Spanish rail operator **Renfe** (www.renfe.com). For domestic routes, Portugal's national train service **CP** (www.cp.pt) runs mainline services to Porto, the Algarve, and other destinations as well as suburban lines around Lisbon.

By Bus
If you aren't in a hurry, the bus can be a cheap alternative for getting to Lisbon from elsewhere in Europe. Europe's largest coach line, **Eurolines** (www.eurolines.com), operates routes to Lisbon from dozens of European cities, including London, Paris, and Madrid.

Getting Around

By Metro
The **Metro** (www.metrolisboa.pt), Lisbon's clean and modern subway, is the quickest and easiest way to get around. The four Metro lines are identified by color: red, yellow, blue and green. Buy a **Viva viagem** card from the booths and machines in the stations. Cards cost just 0.5€ and can be charged up with amounts from 3€ to 40€ through a system called "zapping." Using the card, a single ride costs 1.31€, and the amount is deducted from your card when you touch it on a contact pad as you enter and leave the station platform. The cards can also be used on buses, suburban trains (like those heading to Cascais and Sintra), ferryboats crossing the Tagus river, and Lisbon's iconic trams and funiculars. Many of the Metro stations are clad in tiles decorated by **modern artists** and are attractions in their own right. The Olaias, Parque, and Cidade Universitária stations are particularly recommended.

By Taxi
Taxis are plentiful, relatively cheap, and easily hailed in the street in all but the busiest times. A 15-minute trip from riverside Praça do Comércio to the cool Campo de Ourique neighborhood will cost around 5€, for example. For a radio taxi, call ☎ 21/811-9000 or go to www.retalis.pt. **Uber** and other ride hailing services such as **Taxify** and **Cabify** are available (despite efforts by taxi drivers to shut them down). *Note:* Tipping cab drivers is not obligatory, but most travelers usually round up to the nearest euro, or add a euro or so for longer trips.

By Bus, Train, and Streetcar
Buses can be a fun way to see the city. The city bus company **Carris** (www.carris.pt) runs an extensive network that gets to places the Metro doesn't reach. **Viva viagem** tickets work on buses; just swipe them across the yellow reader when you hop on board. Carris also runs the **streetcar** lines that have become a major attraction for visitors (annoying regular users who often find them too crowded on their commute to work). Other public transport options include **suburban rail lines** departing from Cais do Sodré station for the beach resorts of the Cascais coast and to Sintra from Rossio station. For a cheap, off-the-beaten-track

adventure and great views of Lisbon, take the little orange **ferryboats** to the south bank of the Tagus.

By Car

Driving in the congested, narrow streets of central Lisbon is rarely enjoyable. The compact city center is better explored on foot or by public transport. Consider hiring a car only for excursions to less-accessible places. If you're driving to Lisbon as part of a longer road trip, do what many *Lisboetas* do and keep your car in a garage until it's time to leave the city.

On Foot

Lisbon's city center is best explored on foot, but tackling the hills can be a strain on calf muscles. Combine walking with bus, tram, and streetcar rides. In hot weather, carry plenty of water and do like the locals do: Make plenty of pit stops in the countless cafes. Lisbon also has a growing number of **cycle hire** outlets. Biking is fun along the banks of the Tagus and in flat riverside districts like the Baixa, Santos and Belém, but heading up the cobbled hillsides of Alfama or Chiado is only for the brave or foolhardy.

Fast Facts

APARTMENT RENTALS Short-term rentals have expanded rapidly in Lisbon, with over 13,500 vacation apartments known as **Alojamento Local** registered since 2013. These cater to all budgets, are often in restored historic buildings, and can offer practical city center alternatives to traditional hotels. Check out platforms like **Airbnb.com, HomeAway.com,** and **VRBO.com** to see what's available.

Know, however, that the boom has triggered mixed feelings among *Lisboetas*. Some are pleased that many downtown buildings have been renovated to accommodate vacationers, but there's concern that rents have gone up and local families have been forced out in the process, particularly in picturesque neighborhoods, like Alfama.

ATMS/CASHPOINTS The easiest way to get cash is taking it directly from your bank account in euros by using your debit card at one of Lisbon's more than 3,000 ATMs. Multilingual machines that let you carry out transactions in English are found in shopping malls, railway stations, airports, as well as in banks. If you're coming from outside the euro area, the bank may charge a small commission, around 1% to 3% on the exchange. Rates are less favorable at exchange bureaus and even worse in hotels and stores.

BUSINESS HOURS Banks open Monday through Friday from 8:30am to 3pm. City center **shops** tend to open Monday to Saturday between 9 and 10am until 7 or 8pm. Shopping malls stay open longer, often until 11pm, and are usually open Sundays. Out-of-center stores tend to close around 5 to 6pm as well as on Saturday afternoons and Sundays. Most **museums** are closed Mondays; otherwise they are generally open 10am to 6pm, and smaller ones may break for lunch.

Most **restaurants** serve lunch from noon until 3pm and dinner from 7:30 to 10pm, but it's not hard to find places serving food all day and until midnight or later. On Sundays many restaurants only open for lunch; others take their weekly break on Mondays.

CONSULATES & EMBASSIES **US Embassy,** Avenida das Forças Armadas (☎ 21/727-3300, pt.usembassy.gov); **Canadian Embassy,** Avenida da Liberdade, 196–200, 3rd floor (☎ 21/316-4600, www.canadainternational.gc.ca); **UK Embassy,** Rua de São Bernardo, 33 (☎ 21/392-4000, www.gov.uk); **Australian Embassy,** Avenida da Liberdade, 196–200, 2nd floor (☎ 21/310-1500, www.portugal. embassy.gov.au).

DOCTORS European Union citizens can get access to the National Health Service if they carry a **European Health Insurance Card**. Travelers from elsewhere should contact their insurer to check their coverage. The U.S. embassy has a **list of hospitals and doctors:** (www.pt.usembassy.gov/u-s-citizen-services/doctors). If your insurance provides coverage, Lisbon's best private hospitals include **Hospital da Luz** (www.hospitaldaluz.pt; ☎ 21/710-44-00); **CUF** (www. saudecuf.pt/en; ☎ 21/112-17-17); and **Lusíadas** (www.lusiadas.pt/en; ☎ 21/770-40-40).

ELECTRICITY Portugal uses 200-volt plugs with two round pins like the rest of continental Europe. You'll need a simple converter for devices using flat-pin North American plugs or UK-style three-pin plugs. Most modern appliances are dual-voltage—check to see if they have 110-220 on the plug. If not, you'll need a current converter.

EMERGENCIES For police, ambulance, or firefighters, call ☎ **112.**

GAY & LESBIAN TRAVELERS Portugal was one of the first countries in Europe to outlaw workplace discrimination based on sexual orientation, and it legalized **gay marriage** in 2010. In 2016, gay couples were given equal adoption rights. Overt homophobia and hate crimes are rare. Lisbon has a thriving gay scene. The annual **Pride** festival in June is a major event on the social calendar, and September's **Queer Lisbon** is the city's oldest film festival. The main gay rights organization **ILGA Portugal** (http://ilga-portugal. pt) apologizes for not having all its website translated into English but welcomes calls (☎ **21/887-3918**). Another site offering information for LGTB travelers to Portugal is **www.gay.portugalconfidential**.

HOLIDAYS 1 January (New Year's Day), March/April (Good Friday and Easter Monday), 25 April (Liberty Day), 1 May (Labor Day), May (Corpus Christi), 10 June (National Day), 13 June (St. Anthony's Day—Lisbon only), 15 August (Assumption), 5 October (Republic Day), 1 November (All Saints' Day), 1 December (Independence Day), 8 December (Immaculate Conception), 25 December (Christmas).

INSURANCE For information on traveler's insurance, trip cancellation insurance, and medical insurance while traveling, please visit www.frommers.com/planning.

INTERNET Lisbon is a wired-up country. Most hotels and hostels have free **Wi-Fi** in rooms and public spaces. It's common as well in cafes and restaurants; just ask the staff for the password. You'll also find Wi-Fi in most museums, libraries, railway stations, and other public spaces.

MAIL & POSTAGE Sending postcards and standard letters from Portugal costs 0.75€ to elsewhere in Europe and 0.80€ to the rest of world. Post office opening hours vary, but the bigger branches are usually open from 9am to 6pm. The **CTT** mail company has a list of post offices on its website (www.ctt.pt) and a phone line for enquiries in English (☎ **70-726-2626**).

MONEY Portugal uses the single European currency the **euro** (€), divided into 100 cents. At press time, the exchange rate was approximately 1€ = $1.143 or £0.89. For up-to-the-minute rates, check www.xe.com.

PASSPORTS For visits of less than 3 months, U.S., Canadian, Irish, Australian, New Zealand, or British citizens need only a valid passport to enter Portugal.

PHARMACIES Pharmacies (*farmácias*) are normally open Monday to Friday 9am to 7pm and Saturdays 9am to 1pm. A list of "*farmácias de serviço*" that stay open late and on Sundays are listed in the windows of all pharmacies and on the website: www.farmaciasdeservico.net.

POLICE A "tourist police" unit dealing with travelers' problems is based in the pink Palácio Foz building in Praça dos Restauradores (☎ **21/342-16-23** or 21/340-00-90).

SAFETY Violent crime against tourists is rare, but pickpocketing and theft from parked cars are the biggest problems. Don't leave valuables in cars if you can avoid it, even during daylight. **Pickpockets** and bag snatchers tend to focus on crowded areas where there are lots of tourists. The Chiado district and the Portas do Sol viewpoint in Lisbon are hotspots. They also operate on public transport; take special care on packed Lisbon streetcars. If you are robbed, it's best to report it to the police. They may not put out an all-points alert, but they will return stolen documents, which frequently show up dumped by criminals after they've emptied purses of cash. Foreigners are frequently approached by shady characters offering **cocaine** or **marijuana**. What they sell is usually fake. These characters can be intimidating and seem to operate with impunity. It's best to politely say "no" and walk away.

SMOKING Smoking is banned in most public buildings and on transport. Under certain conditions, restaurants and bars can set aside smoking rooms, and hotels can assign up to 40% of rooms for smokers. The rules are generally applied strictly in restaurants, less so in some bars. If you want to dine or drink alfresco, be aware that many smokers head to outside tables to escape the ban.

TAXES Sales tax, known as **IVA,** is included in the price of almost everything you buy in Portugal. The standard rate is 23%, although reduced rates apply to some purchases. In restaurants, for example, the rate on food is 13%, but on booze the full 23% applies. Your receipt should tell you how much you've given the government. Residents outside the EU can get a **sales tax refund** on purchases they are taking home over 50€ to 60€, depending on the type of product. Look for stores displaying tax-free shopping signs and ask them for a refund form. You can get the tax refunded at the airport when you leave. For more details, check out www.premiertaxfree.com or www.globalblue.com.

Taxes are usually included in the price of your hotel room, but City Hall has controversially introduced a special "**tourism tax,**" meaning that 1€ per person per night is added to your hotel bill, up to a maximum of 7€. It does not apply to children under 13.

TIPPING Service charges are only occasionally included in restaurant bills, but **tipping is optional.** In posh places, people may leave up to 10%; elsewhere rarely more than 5% and only then if you've appreciated the service. Often people will just drop a couple of coins or nothing. In bars and cafes it's rare to tip more than a few coins. In taxis, too, tipping is optional, although people will often round up the bill to the nearest euro or two; likewise with hair dressers or barbers. In hotels with porters or valet parking, you might want to tip them 0.50€ or 1€.

TOILETS Public toilets are rare. If you are caught short, nip into a cafe, buy an espresso, and ask for the *casa de banho.* Bathrooms are labeled *homens* for men and *senhoras* for women.

TOURIST INFORMATION The main office on Praça do Comércio (☎ 21/031-2810) is open daily 9am to 8pm. The city has nine other "Ask Me Lisboa" offices and kiosks, including at the airport. See list at **www.visitlisbon.com**.

TOURS A vast array of tours is available, from **hop-on, hop-off circuits** on double-decker buses (www.yellowbustours.com) to **tasting tours** with culinary insiders (www.culinarybackstreets.com) to **bike rides** along the Tagus river or **tuk-tuks** that weave among the narrow lanes.

TRAVELERS WITH DISABILITIES With its steep hills and narrow cobbled sidewalks, Lisbon can be challenging for people with disabilities. See **Portugal Acessível.**

(www.portugalacessivel.beta.due.pt) for listings in English on the accessibility of hotels, museums, beaches, and other sites. Half of the buses with **Carris bus company** (www.carris.pt/en/reduced-mobility) are adapted for wheelchairs. Carris also has special minibuses for special-needs passengers (must be reserved 2 days in advance; ☎ 21/361-31-41). Lisbon's **Metro** stations have wide-access gates for disabled customers and ticket vending machines adapted for visually impaired users. Currently, 36 of its 56 stations offer full accessibility.

Lisbon: A Brief History

138 B.C. Romans incorporate the city of Felicitas Julia Olisipo into their empire after conquering the Iberian Peninsula.

5TH–6TH C. A.D. German tribes occupy the city, calling it *Ulishbona.*

714 Muslim invaders from North Africa take the city, naming it *Al-Ushbuna.*

1147 After several attempts, Christian forces take the city under Afonso Henriques, first king of Portugal. He's helped by crusaders from northern Europe.

1256 King Afonso III makes Lisbon capital of Portugal.

1290 King Diniz founds the university.

1373 Lisbon sacked by Spanish forces from the Kingdom of Castile.

1386 Portugal and England sign the Treaty of Windsor, the world's oldest surviving diplomatic alliance.

1415 Prince Henry the Navigator conquers Ceuta in North Africa, launching Lisbon's role as capital of a maritime empire.

1444 First Africans sold as slaves by Portugal; over the next 4 centuries Portuguese ships will carry millions to bondage, mainly in Brazil.

1497 Vasco da Gama sails from Lisbon to India, opening up trade routes to Asia and turning Lisbon into a global trade center.

1500 Pedro Alvares Cabral discovers Brazil.

1501 Work begins on the Jerónimos Monastery.

1506 Catholic mobs massacre around 2,000 Jews.

1540 The Inquisition holds the first *auto da fé* in Rossio Square trying and executing people of Jewish heritage.

1580 Spain takes control of Portugal two years after King Sebastian dies without an heir in a failed attempt to conquer Morocco.

1588 Spanish Armada sails from Lisbon in doomed bid to invade England.

1640 Spanish ousted by uprising by Portuguese nobles who ultimately triumph in war to restore independence.

1706 King João V takes the throne. He undertakes a lavish building program funded by gold shipped from Brazil.

1755 Earthquake, tsunami, and fires destroy much of Lisbon in western Europe's deadliest natural disaster. Up to 100,000 killed. The Marquês de Pombal leads the reconstruction, founding the Baixa district.

1807 Napoleon troops capture Lisbon in the first of three French invasions before they are eventual driven out of Portugal in 1813 with the help of British forces under the Duke of Wellington.

1822 Brazil becomes independent.

1828 Portugal weakened by civil war that lasts 6 years before victory of liberal over conservative forces.

1856 First railway line is built between Lisbon and Carregado.

1901 Lisbon's electric streetcars start running.

1908 Gunmen assassinate King Carlos and his oldest son, Praça do Comercio.

1910 Monarchy overthrown and republic declared.

1916 Portugal joins WWI on side of the allies.

1926 Military coup topples the republic.

1932 António de Oliveira Salazar takes power, imposing the Fascist-inspired *Estado Novo* dictatorship that will last over 4 decades.

1961/2 Lisbon's Benfica soccer team win European Champions Cup 2 years running.

1966 Engineers from San Francisco help build a suspension bridge to span the Tagus and give Lisbon its first road link across the river.

1974 On April 25th, the peaceful Carnation Revolution topples the dictatorship and ushers in democracy.

1975 First democratic elections in 50 years. Hundreds of thousands of refugees flood into Lisbon as Portugal's African colonies are granted independence.

1986 Portugal joins the EU.

1998 Lisbon hosts Expo '98 in the newly built Parque das Nações district symbolizing economic dynamism.

2015 Lisbon's emergence as a major tourism destination gives the city a facelift and helps revive Portugal's economy after years of recession.

Useful Phrases

Useful Words & Phrases

ENGLISH	PORTUGUESE	PRONUNCIATION
Good day	Bom dia	bom-dee-ah
How are you?	Como está?	kohm shtah
Very well	Muito bem	moy-to bey-m
Thank you	Obrigado/a	o-bree-gah-doh /dah
You're welcome	De nada	deh nah-dah
Goodbye	Adeus	ah-day-oosh
Please	Por favor/Faz favor	por fah-vohr/fash fah-vohr
Yes	Sim	si-(m)
No	Não	now
Excuse me	Desculpe	deh-shkoolp
Where is . . . ?	Onde fica ...?	ohn-day fee-kah...?
To the right	À direito	ah deer-eh-toh
To the left	À esquerda	ah esh-kair-dah
I would like . . .	Eu gostaria...	eh-ooh gosh-tah-ree-ya
I want . . .	Quero...	kair-roh...
Do you have . . . ?	Tem?	Tay-m?
How much is it?	Quanto é?	kwahn-toh eh?
When?	Quando?	kwahn-doh?
What?	Como? / O quê?	Coh-moh? / oh-keh?
Yesterday	Ontem	ohn-tey-m
Today	Hoje	ohj
Tomorrow	Amanhã	ah-mah-nyah-ah
Good	Bom/Boa	boh-m/bo-a
Bad	Mau/Má	m-owh/mah
Better (Best)	(O) melhor	(oh) meh-ly-ohr
More	Mais	my-sh
Less	Menos	meh-nohs/meh-nyus
Do you speak English?	Fala inglês?	Fah-lah eeng-gleysh?
I don't understand	Não percebo	now pair-seb-oh
What time is it?	Que horas são?	keh oh-rahsh s-owh
The check, please	À conta, faz favor	ah con-tah fash fah-vohr
The station	À estação	ah es-tah-saoh
a hotel	um hotel	oom oh-tehl
the market	o mercado	oh mehr-kah-doh
restaurant	um restaurante	oom rehs-tow-rahnt
the toilet	a casa do banho	ah casa doh ban-yo
a doctor	um médico	oon meh-dee-koh
the road	a estrada	ah esh-trah-dah
to eat	comer	ko-mehr
a room	um quarto	oom quah-toh
a book	um livro	oom lee-vroh
a dictionary	um dicionário	oom dik-syoh-nah-ryoh

Numbers

NUMBER	PORTUGUESE	PRONUNCIATION
1	um	oom
2	dois	doysh
3	três	tresh
4	quatro	kwah-troh
5	cinco	sink-oh
6	seis	saysh
7	sete	set
8	oito	oy-toh
9	nove	nov
10	dez	desh
11	onze	onz
12	doze	doz
13	treze	treh-z
14	catorze	kah-tohr-z
15	quinze	kin-z
16	dezasseis	dez-ah-saysh
17	dezassete	dez-ah-set
18	dezoito	dez-oy-to
19	dezanove	dez-ah-nov
20	vinte	vint
30	trinta	trin-tah
40	quarenta	kwah-rehn-tah
50	cinquenta	sing-kwehn-tah
60	sessenta	seh-sehn-tah
70	setenta	seh-tehn-tah
80	oitenta	oy-tehn-tah
90	noventa	noh-behn-tah
100	cem	cey-m

Glossary

avenida avenue
azulejos tiles
capela chapel
casa house
castelo castle
igreja church
jardim garden
miradouro viewpoint
mosteiro monastery

museu museum
parque park
praça/largo square
rio river
rua street
sé cathedral
teatro theater
torre tower

Index

See also Accommodations and Restaurant Indexes

Photo **Credits**